RECONCILIATION
A guiding vision
for South Africa?

EDITOR

Ernst M. Conradie

SERIES EDITOR

Renier Koegelenberg

SUN PRESS

EFSA SERIES | ECUMENICAL AND DEVELOPMENT PERSPECTIVES

Reconciliation: A guiding vision for South Africa?

Copyright © 2013 EFSA and authors

First edition 2013

ISBN 978-1-920689-08-7 (Print)
ISBN 978-1-920689-09-4 (ePub)

Set in 10.5/13 Palatino Linotype
Typesetting and conversion: Johannes Richter

SUN PRESS is an imprint of SUN MeDIA Stellenbosch. Academic, professional and reference works are published under this imprint in print and electronic format. This publication may be ordered directly from www.sun-e-shop.co.za.

Produced by SUN MeDIA Stellenbosch.

www.africansunmedia.co.za
www.sun-e-shop.co.za

Ecumenical Foundation of Southern Africa (EFSA)

Executive Chairperson, Prof. H. Russel Botman
Executive Director, Dr Renier A. Koegelenberg
Postal address: P.O. Box 3103, Matieland, Stellenbosch, 7602, South Africa
Physical address: 24-26 Longifolia Street, Paradyskloof, Stellenbosch

Office of the Executive Director
Phone: +27 (0)21 880-1734
Fax.: +27 (0)21 880-1735
Fax.: +27 (0)86 768-4121
Mobile: +27 (0)83 625-1047
E-mail: efsa@cddc.co.za
Websites: http://www.efsa-institute.org.za
http://www.nrasd.org.za

ACKNOWLEDGEMENTS

EFSA gratefully acknowledges the following institutions for their support of this publication:

- Die Evangelische Kirche in Deutschland (EKD)
- Brot für die Welt
- University of the Western Cape, Department of Religion and Theology

EFSA

INSTITUTE FOR THEOLOGICAL & INTERDISCIPLINARY RESEARCH

Ecumenical Foundation of Southern Africa (EFSA)

The EFSA Institute, founded in 1990, is an independent ecumenical institute that functions as a division of the non-profitable "Cape Development and Dialogue Centre Trust" (CDDC). Trustees include Dr Welile Mazamisa, Archbishop Dr Thabo Makgoba, Dr André van Niekerk, Prof. Russel Botman and Dr Renier Koegelenberg. It consists of a unique network of participating institutions: representatives of the Faculties of Theology and the Departments of Religious Studies of the Universities in the Western Cape are represented on the Board and Executive of the EFSA Institute.

Generally speaking, the EFSA Institute attempts to promote consensus between different sectors, interest groups and stakeholders on the challenges and problems facing our society. It strives to play a facilitating role by providing a platform for public debate, even of controversial issues.

Both in its structure and function there is a dialectic tension between an academic (research-based) approach and the need to address specific needs of the church and other religious communities. This tension is embedded in the main issues facing the churches in our society. In a general sense the EFSA Institute tries to focus public attention (and the attention of the church or academic institutions) on specific problems in society.

Currently, the focus is on the following priorities.

Firstly, the *development role of the church* and other religious communities: the eradication of poverty in South Africa; the role of religious networks in community development, in social and welfare services; and the development of community and youth leadership.

Secondly, the *healing and reconciliatory role of the church* and other religious communities: this includes a project on the role of women in the healing of our violent society; the mobilisation of the church and religious communities against crime and violence; and the breaking down of stereotypes (racism) in our society.

Thirdly, the *formation of values in the strengthening of a moral society by the church* and other religious communities: the promotion of moral values such as honesty; support for the weak; respect for life and human rights.

Fourthly, the *development of youth and community leadership*: special courses for the development of leadership skills among our youth have been developed and are presented to support the building of a new society.

It is also significant that the EFSA Institute acts as Secretariat to the National Religious Association for Social Development (NRASD), which is a Principal Recipient of the Global Fund to Fight AIDS, Tuberculosis and Malaria in South Africa. It is also a partner of Johns Hopkins Health and Education in South Africa (JHHESA – a USAID funded programme). It currently serves as the national secretariat of the religious sector – for the South African National Aids Council (SANAC).

These priorities cannot be separated from one another, since many of the complex social issues are interrelated.

Dr Renier A Koegelenberg
Executive Director

CONTENTS

FOREWORD

The editor of this collection of essays emphasises that "the aim ... is not to address any one of the substantive issues related to reconciliation, national unity or social cohesion in the South African context. It does not seek, for example, to assess the legacy of the South African Truth and Reconciliation Commission. Instead, its purpose is conceptual clarification for the sake of theological reflection."

The contributions highlight the tension between the way that the term "reconciliation" is used in society and its different meanings within the Christian discourse on reconciliation.

In his overview the editor refers to a comment by Beyers Naudé (in Hansen 2005:40):

> The concept of reconciliation also implies very clearly that to God this was meant not only as a verbal message to man, but that it had to become incarnate; an audible word that had to become a visible deed in the flesh before reconciliation could be effective. This was the price God was willing to pay – the Incarnation of Christ was the Reconciliation of God with man. Do we realize what this implies: that all talk of reconciliation remains meaningless and even becomes dangerous if words are not transformed into deeds?
>
> Do we realize that our confession of faith becomes nothing but cheap talk, yes, becomes an act of hypocrisy if we do not fully accept and enact the reconciliation of God in our lives?

The contributors' reflections on the meaning of reconciliation are not only part of our ongoing biblical interpretation, but also entails wrestling with the meaning and significance of reconciliation in our own situation.

Renier Koegelenberg

INTRODUCTION

The Department of Religion and Theology at the University of the Western Cape is hosting a series of think tanks on the interface between ecumenical theology and social ethics in the (South) African context. It has identified a number of themes where some degree of clarity may aid further ecumenical discourse. These think tanks will be hosted over a three-year period from October 2012 to June 2015. Reflections emerging from these think tanks will be published in cooperation with the EFSA Institute in a series of booklets – where appropriate. The themes that are envisaged include the following:

- Guiding visions for the transition to a post-apartheid society;
- A critical assessment of "reconciliation" as one of the guiding visions during and beyond the transition period;
- Notions and forms of "ecumenicity" in (South) Africa;
- The quest for denominational identity within mainline churches;
- Ecumenical engagement in the form of NGOs and FBOs as dynamos for social transformation in the Western Cape;
- Religion and moral formation towards responsible citizenship;
- Recognising current ecclesial reforming/deforming movements in South Africa;
- African Pentecostal expressions of ecumenicity in (South) Africa;
- African notions of leadership;
- Ecclesiology and ethics in the (South) African context: how are ecumenical studies related to social ethics?

The first of the themes indicated above focused on a number of guiding concepts for social transformation in the South African context. These were juxtaposed in relation to the South African government's National Planning Commission's document entitled "National Development Plan: Vision for 2030" as the vision for social transformation articulated by those who are currently in a position of political power in South Africa. This notion of a guiding concept for social transformation requires extensive further clarification. The following interim definitions may be offered here.

- Guiding concepts to describe a vision for social transformation are operational concepts are (tacitly) employed by groups in positions of political, military and economic power (for example, at a national level) to guide a process of social transformation over longer periods of time. They do not only describe penultimate or ultimate aims, but also indicate what is needed to get there. In that sense they are indeed operational concepts. They can typically be captured in single words or crisp phrases.

- These guiding concepts respond to (perceived) needs and problems in the current social order on the basis of social analysis. This indicates the need for social transformation (used here in a generic and neutral sense allowing for progression but also retrogression).

- These guiding concepts recognise some obstacles or threats that hinder or undermine the possibility for rapid social transformation. This is why they have to be operational concepts to guide the process of overcoming such obstacles. The hindrances may be captured under generic (often religious) categories such as hubris, domination (oppression), greed (selfishness, entitlement), sloth and alienation, or in structural terms such as capitalist exploitation, consumerism, moral failure and the disintegration of the social fabric.

- All these guiding concepts (have to) respond to a number of penultimate aims/goals/values such human dignity (*ubuntu*), the basic human rights that follow from that, equality, justice, peace, liberty, progress, democracy (a participatory society), sustainability, civilisation, being educated, enlightenment, skills development towards employment, reaching maturity and so forth (in no particular order). These operational concepts may be described as guiding concepts because they guide current processes of social transformation towards these penultimate goals by indicating certain priorities. For that reason the phrases employed require unpacking in relation to a range of other concepts.

- These guiding concepts also respond to ultimate goals that are typically articulated in religious or quasi-religious categories including a rich array of metaphors and symbols.

- These guiding concepts employed to describe a vision for social transformation are always contested precisely because they indicate certain priorities amidst several penultimate goals and because they are based on a contestable social analysis of current needs and obstacles or threats. As a result in every epoch there are alternative proposals to capture a vision for social transformation. These may be articulated by emerging power blocks that are dominant in their own sphere of influence but not (yet) at a national level. They may also be articulated by those on the margins of political and economic power, but who nevertheless exercise some influence in public debate.

"Reconciliation" may be regarded as one of these guiding concepts for social transformation that gained a certain priority, especially in the period between 1990 and 1994. It was also prominent during the proceedings of the South African Truth and Reconciliation Commission (1996-1998), albeit that the possibility and even desirability of such reconciliation was also highly contested. Although the many manifestations of conflict and violence in South Africa remain undeniable, it is by no means obvious that renewed calls for (national) reconciliation would be symbolically appropriate. The symbol of reconciliation was highly contested in the 1980s and remains highly contested in the current South African context (see Smit 1986).

The think tanks hosted by the Department of Religion and Theology at UWC are structured in the form of the presentation of an invited position paper followed by responses and extensive discussions. This structure is reflected in the contributions included in this booklet. The position paper was produced by Ernst Conradie in conversation with colleagues and postgraduate students in the Department of Religion and Theology at UWC. The responses and other contributions by Mary Burton, Fanie du Toit, Sarah Hills, Demaine Solomons and Vuyani Vellem follow.

These reflections are made available for wider ecumenical discussion through collaboration with the Ecumenical Foundation of Southern Africa, a long-standing partner of the Department of Religion and Theology at UWC.

Ernst M. Conradie (Editor)

1

RECONCILIATION AS ONE GUIDING VISION FOR SOUTH AFRICA?

Conceptual Analysis and Theological Reflection

Ernst M. Conradie

Why reconciliation?

The term "reconciliation" has been one of the guiding concepts in Christian discourse in the South African context at least since the publication of the famous *Message to the People of South Africa* in 1968. In the 1980s the term was used in conflicting ways in the Belhar Confession, the Kairos Document and the National Initiative for Reconciliation. Christians played a leading role in the planning for and proceedings of the Truth and Reconciliation Commission in the 1990s. Since that time it is often used to offer theological reflection on social conflict in South Africa and elsewhere in the world.[1] Although it is no longer one of the dominant concepts (such as "liberation", economic "growth", "reconstruction" and "development") to guide a vision for South Africa in the post-apartheid era (towards 2030), it still forms part of the ongoing discourse in this regard.

The purpose of this contribution is to aid continued theological reflection on the basis of a conceptual analysis of the different ways in which the term is used in a Christian context. This also requires reflection on the distinct ways in which the term is used in everyday life, in South African society and in discourses on mediation and conflict resolution. The

---

1   For a detailed account of how the term was used in the South African context in the 20th century, see De Gruchy (2002:30-43).

purpose of this contribution is at least partly related to the work of a number of postgraduate students in the Department of Religion and Theology at the University of the Western Cape, who are working on aspects of reconciliation and require some conceptual clarification to proceed with their studies.[2]

It should be noted here that the validity of the term 'reconciliation' as one expression of a guiding vision for the transition to a post-apartheid South Africa is not addressed in this contribution. It is simply assumed that this term has played a significant albeit ambiguous role. The truth is that the term has been highly contested at least since the 1980s.

• Consider in this regard Dirkie Smit's (1986:88) doubts over the potential of the symbol of reconciliation to transform society, since the term "needs clarification, and the moment that an idea needs to be clarified, it has already lost its power as a symbol. A symbol is precisely something that needs no explanation, but is self-evident and immediately grips the imagination. Because of this, people frequently find it necessary to speak of 'true' or 'real' or 'authentic' reconciliation, thereby already implying that they reject some other kind of reconciliation, which is 'cheap' or 'false'."

• The Kairos Document (1985) denounced the prioritising of reconciliation as "church theology". It famously maintained that "it would be totally unChristian to plead for reconciliation and peace before the present injustices have been removed. Any such plea plays into the hands of the oppressor by trying to persuade those of us who are oppressed to accept our oppression and to become reconciled to the intolerable crimes that are committed against us. That is not Christian reconciliation, it is sin. It is asking us to become accomplices in our own oppression, to become servants of the devil. No reconciliation is possible in South Africa without

---

2   This contribution is the product of ongoing discussions with postgraduate students, often in the context of developing research proposals. It has also been discussed and critiqued at a departmental seminar where my colleagues and other students raised valuable questions. Insights emerging from these discussions were continuously incorporated into the document over an extended period of time. I wish to acknowledge the specific inputs from Robert Agyarko, Craig Arendse, Lerato Kobe, Edward Mwansa, Mbhekeni Nkosi, Ayanda Ntuli, Demaine Solomons and Christo Zimri, among several others. The document remains work in progress and may not ever be completed, given the scope of the available literature. There is always another aspect that may be added.

justice."[3] It was argued that good and evil cannot and should not be reconciled with one another. "Liberation" instead of "reconciliation" was typically used in this context.

- Black theologians such as Itumeleng Mosala (1987) and Tinyiko Maluleke (1999) went further by arguing that the primary need is not for reconciliation between black people and white people in South Africa: "Our alienation is not alienation from white people first and foremost. Our alienation is from our land, our cattle, our labour which is objectified in industrial machines and technological instrumentation. Our reconciliation with white people will follow from our reconciliation with our fundamental means of livelihood" (Maluleke 1999:103). Maluleke thus rejects "integrationist reconciliation", understood as the operationalising of multiracial ideologies and theologies aimed at combating white racism. This amounts to the integration of "non-whites" into liberal agendas (Maluleke 1999:101-102).

- Understandably, there is widespread scepticism over what may be regarded as shallow or "cheap" reconciliation (see Bosch 1986:161). Moreover, as Miguez Bonino observes, "The ideological appropriation of the Christian doctrine of reconciliation by the liberal capitalist system in order to conceal the brutal fact of class and imperialist exploitation and conflict is one – if not the – major heresy of our time" (quoted by Mkwatshwa 1986:68). Gregory Baum comments that conservative Catholic bishops in Latin America accused liberation theologians of setting the poor against the affluent, thus sinning against the unity of the church. Instead, they proposed a theology of reconciliation in which all people are called to repentance and forgiveness in order to find unity in Christ: "They preach a reconciliation that does not demand structural change in the social order; their theology allows the rich to keep their power and privilege" (in Baum & Wells 1997:188).

- Consider also the widespread and lasting scepticism among many South Africans over the impact of the proceedings of the Truth and Reconciliation Commission. It may well be that after almost two decades of democracy the impulse for retribution is still stronger than the impulse for reconciliation.[4] Accordingly, the leadership offered by Archbishop Tutu towards reconciliation based on forgiveness is "setting the bar too high" for most ordinary South Africans, who remain disillusioned with social transformation in South Africa.

---

3 See *The Kairos Document: Challenge to the church*, revised second edition (1986:9). Robert Schreiter (1992:25) therefore insists that "liberation is the necessary precondition for reconciliation".

4 This is an open question raised by Jonathan Jansen as quoted in Boesak & DeYoung (2012:106).

- Curtiss DeYoung (2012:23) comments that reconciliation is often understood in the United States to imply that institutions led by whites have to add or include people of colour without recognising the need for a transformation of such institutions towards a truly inclusive humanity.

- Likewise, as Du Toit (1998:viii) observes, "It is difficult not to be sceptical about the initiatives that white mainline churches will take to further the reconciliation process." Indeed, the often quoted observation that Sunday 10h00 remains the "most divided hour" of the week in terms of culture and ethnicity (not only in South Africa) suggests a scepticism as to whether Christianity has the credibility to play any meaningful role in national reconciliation. The manifold divisions in Christianity are obvious for the world to see – not only in terms of race and gender, but also in terms of denominational differences, the role of the laity, attitudes towards sexual orientation and a range of other ethical concerns.

- Finally, even advocates of reconciliation recognise its elusive nature (see Villa-Vicencio 2002:3), that "we are searching for a concept that defies clarity" (Weinstein 2011:7), and hence many nowadays opt instead for reflection on degrees of social cohesion.[5] Or, according to Jakes Gerwel (2000:284), one should avoid confusion between politics and religion, since this may pathologise what is relatively healthy by demanding the perpetual quest for the holy grail of reconciliation. Instead, what is needed is a "commitment to consensus seeking, cultivation of conventions of civility and respect for contracts".

Nevertheless, the term reconciliation is still widely used in everyday language and also in secular contexts. If anything, the elusive nature of reconciliation has helped Christians to recognise its eschatological character. "Radical reconciliation" (Boesak & DeYoung 2012) is indeed a regulative ideal that can challenge shallow or cheap forms of social cohesion.

The purpose of this contribution is *not* to suggest that the symbol of reconciliation be prioritised in South African discourse or to maintain it as a moral demand, but to seek as much conceptual clarity as may be achieved with respect to such an elusive concept. Given the

---

5   In the words of Weinstein (2011:7): "Instead of focusing on reconciliation, I suggest we consider the idea that, as a starting point, living together peacefully without overt violence may be enough; that anything more than that is years, perhaps generations, away."

vast literature on concepts[6] such as reconciliation, forgiveness, justice and restitution from a wide array of disciplines (including conflict studies, law, philosophy, political studies, psychology, theology), any conceptual analysis will remain preliminary and subject to multiple corrections, if not dispute. This contribution may therefore be overly bold and therefore contentious, but at least it seeks to respond to the need for conceptual clarity.

It should also be noted that the aim of this contribution is not to address any one of the substantive issues related to reconciliation, national unity or social cohesion in the South African context. It does not seek, for example, to assess the legacy of the South African Truth and Reconciliation Commission. Instead, its purpose is conceptual clarification for the sake of theological reflection and therefore remains at a high level of abstraction.

What does reconciliation mean in a Christian context?

The problem underlying conceptual clarification is that the term "reconciliation" is used in quite different ways in society. It is commonly used with respect to personal relationships that have become distorted in marriage or family life, or between neighbours, colleagues or members of an organisation. In such relationships some form of reconciliation is regarded as necessary to avoid unwanted tension and conflict, and perhaps to allow the relationship to flourish again. In a socio-political context the term is used in a weaker sense, namely to describe perceptions, attitudes and behaviour of individuals and groups towards other social groups – whether or not knowledge of individuals in that social group is required or not. These groups are typically defined in terms of markers such as race, class, gender, language, culture, nationality, religious

---

6   "Reconciliation" is used in this contribution as an umbrella concept that includes concepts such as forgiveness, justice and restitution. The inverse is possible, namely to include elements of reconciliation in the quest for justice. The exercise may therefore be contested on the grounds of prioritising reconciliation in this way. Moreover, umbrella concepts tend to become all-inclusive and therefore vague, if not meaningless. In response to such caveats, this contribution may be understood as an attempt to extend a conceptual analysis as far as this may be possible before the exercise will almost inevitably begin to unravel.

affiliation or sexual orientation. The term "reconciliation" is thus used as a barometer for social cohesion, to establish how members of such groups respect, cooperate, get along, tolerate or avoid open conflict with each other.

In a Christian context the term is also used in such ways, of course, but at least three additional layers of meaning may be identified in Christian discourse on reconciliation:

- Reconciliation with God following alienation as a result of what is re-described as "sin", understood as a broken, radically distorted relationship with God;
- Reconciliation through being one with Christ in the body of Christ (the church);
- The ministry of reconciliation through the Holy Spirit in church and society.

This raises the question of how the use of the term reconciliation inside the church is related to the ways it is used outside of a Christian context. Furthermore, one may also reflect on the ways in which the relatedness of these theological, ecclesial and social layers of meaning is understood. For example, what is the relationship between the politics of national reconciliation (e.g. in the 1990s in South Africa) and the Christian doctrine of reconciliation? It would be disastrous to separate these three layers of meaning, but it would be equally problematic to fuse them and thus to confuse the different genres (De Gruchy 2002:24f).

This question is the subject of much theological debate. It raises classic theological questions on the relationship between God and the world, text and context, church and society, and also faith and science. Moreover, these three layers of meaning bring into play all three articles of the Christian confession in relation to each other.

Some would employ a "deductive" logic moving from reconciliation with God to the ministry of reconciliation in society.[7] They would

---

7   According to this logic, the fruits of reconciliation are dependent upon reconciliation with God, taking place in the innermost heart of the one who was lost and found. In the words of John Paul II: "But it has to be added that this reconciliation with God leads, as it were, to other reconciliations which repair

insist that no lasting solution to social conflict can be found without addressing the deepest roots of such social conflict, namely alienation from God. This can only happen through God's gracious forgiveness of sin. Such forgiveness is appropriated through justification, sanctification and the vocation of believers, to adopt classic Reformed language as an example of such views. Such reconciliation in Christ enables and requires reconciliation with one's brothers and sisters in Christ ("We are all one in Christ"). Although the church of Jesus Christ was characterised by a conflicting diversity from the beginning (there were Zealots and tax collectors amongst the 12 disciples), the fellowship of former slaves and slave owners, rich and poor, men and women, those who regarded themselves as ritually pure and lepers could be portrayed as a sign of the possibility of reconciliation in Christ. Indeed, the church may constitute what David Bosch (1975) described as "an alternative community". There can be little doubt about the social significance of such ecclesial forms of reconciliation – as recognised most pertinently in the Belhar Confession of 1982/1986. If anything, this is illustrated by cases where the absence of ecclesial unity proved disastrous – including apartheid South Africa and the complicity of churches in the genocide in Rwanda (see Linden 1997).

According to a "deductive logic", the ministry of reconciliation in church and society only becomes possible on this basis of reconciliation in Christ. The task of this ministry cannot merely be to help people to get along better. Its focus has to remain reconciliation with God. Only then can the deepest roots of social conflict be resolved. Without that, reconciliation in society will always remain inauthentic, shallow, misplaced and vulnerable to renewed conflict. The need for reconciliation in society springs from the celebration of the Holy Communion. The power of such deductive logic is epitomised by the Confession of Belhar: because of God's work of reconciliation in Jesus Christ, Christians cannot accept a social system that assumes the fundamental irreconcilability of people.

---

the breaches caused by sin. The forgiven penitent is reconciled with himself in his innermost being, where he regains his own true identity. He is reconciled with his brethren whom he has in some way attacked and wounded. He is reconciled with the church. He is reconciled with all creation" (quoted in Hay 1998:92).

By contrast, others would suggest that this deductive logic does not account for the process behind the conclusion that was reached, namely that the deepest roots of social conflict lie in human alienation from God. That conclusion could only be reached through contextual and pastoral reflection on such conflict. It is the result of prior analysis, namely recognising that sin constitutes the deepest roots of the human predicament. They would therefore suggest an "inductive" logic where situations of social conflict form the starting point for multi-disciplinary reflection.[8] Theological perspectives may be offered as contributions to such reflection and may be regarded as valuable, if indeed they can deepen a common understanding of what is at stake. They can aid reflection by situating personal and social relationships within a wider, cosmic frame of reference. If not, it may at least be regarded as appropriate to help Christians to come to terms with such conflict amongst themselves. Such theological perspectives would be limited in the sense that they would not necessarily apply to those outside a Christian sphere of influence.

The need for such a wider frame of reference follows the intuition that any breach in a relationship has wider implications than those for the two parties concerned. If such a breach has almost cosmic ramifications, the final resolution of such conflict has to take into account the widest possible scope of the problem. The conclusion is then that reconciliation between two individuals is only possible if the whole of society is reconciled with itself. For that, an ultimate perspective is required: ultimately, reconciliation between two individuals is only possible through reconciliation with God. This invites reflection on the cosmic scope of God's work of reconciliation. Not only human beings or human societies, but the whole created order is included in God's work of reconciliation in Christ. Reconciliation has to be understood in the context of both God's work of creation and of salvation. What is at stake is the tension between Creator and creature that has emerged because

---

8   This distinction draws on an analysis employed by David Bosch in Chapter 5 of his work *Witness to the World* (1980). Bosch admits that this is a tenuous distinction in need of clarification, but opts for the so-called inductive approach, if only because it is more honest than the deductive approach in explaining how the "principles" employed have been identified.

of captivity to the principalities and powers of this world (Col 1:18-23). Thus: "God's cosmic reconciling activity precedes and provides the framework within which God's reconciliation of humanity occurs" (De Gruchy 2002:53).

It should be clear that quite a lot is at stake here. Embedded in the so-called deductive approach is the danger of using abstract theological language, focusing on the church more than on social needs, valuing theological legitimacy more than social relevance. The danger is one of giving revealed answers to questions that few have asked. Embedded in the so-called inductive approach is the danger of self-secularisation, of reducing the Christian confession to nothing more than an example of religious affiliation that may be tolerated as long as its particular claims are not foregrounded. The danger is one of being socially relevant without having anything distinct to offer in response to the situation.

Nevertheless, these two approaches need not be in conflict. Perhaps a constant interplay is called for, precisely because the conclusion of the one may serve as the point of departure for the other. In this contribution the so-called inductive approach (for want of a better term) is followed for the sake of honesty and given the aim of seeking conceptual clarification. The contribution thus commences with conceptual analysis and continuously raises the question of how the symbol of reconciliation is extended to theological language about the relationship between God and the world (especially through the use of footnotes). The three specifically theological ways in which the term is used will again be addressed in the final section of this contribution.

The many faces of reconciliation in society

The term reconciliation may be used with respect to different kinds of relationships. These can be more or less intimate, narrower or broader in scope. Any relationship between two individuals is of course embedded in a complex network of other relationships in families, institutions, communities and in the wider society. This is important to recognise, if only because what reconciliation might entail would not be the same for all cases. It depends on the nature of the prior relationship. Consider the following very different contexts in which the term reconciliation is used in secular contexts:

- Reconciliation between two individuals who have known each other previously (e.g. spouses, parents and children, neighbours, colleagues, former friends);

- Reconciliation following a breach in a formal contract between two individuals who may or may not have had a close prior relationship with each other (e.g. over building contracts, services rendered, purchasing second-hand goods), that is, a relationship based on rights and obligations;[9]

- Reconciliation between individual fellow citizens who may not have known each other prior to an incident that led to animosity (e.g. in the case of road accidents, theft, rape);

- Reconciliation amidst tensions in smaller groups (e.g. in nuclear or extended families, colleagues in a task group, members of a sports team) with a complex set of possible relationships, influenced by an intricate history of prior interactions (logically, one can analyse 25 possible relationships amongst only four individuals);

- Reconciliation between an individual and representatives of an institution, especially over goods and services that were not delivered satisfactorily and/or payment that was not made (e.g. customers being unhappy with a product purchased, clients who are unsatisfied about the way complaints have been addressed, students who are unhappy with the quality of teaching offered);

- Reconciliation between factions in institutions (businesses, schools, sports clubs, town councils, congregations) with equally complex networks of relationships, albeit that the relationship between any two individuals would tend to be shallower;

---

9 Brümmer (2005) distinguishes between such a relationship based on rights and obligations and a form of relationship characterised by reciprocal fellowship. He argues that the terms "forgiveness" and "reconciliation" are best used only with reference to such fellowship. By contrast, the term "reconciliation" is used here with reference to the full spectrum of possible relationships and not only intimate personal fellowship between individuals. One may therefore speak of reconciliation as the continuation of a prior relationship with the problems currently experienced resolved. This may be between workers and management, between law firms suing each other, between rival sports clubs or countries at war with each other. Intimacy is therefore not necessarily a characteristic of reconciliation.

- Reconciliation between representatives of two or more institutions over conflicting interests between these institutions (e.g. legal claims addressed by one company to another);

- Reconciliation in larger but still more or less local communities (e.g. factions in neighbourhoods, rival gangs, rival political parties, racial groups, workers and management,[10] municipal authorities and sectors of the community);

- Reconciliation between larger sectors within the same society that have come into confrontation with each other as a result of structural injustices and maladjustments in the social order (e.g. in the form of racism, xenophobia, tensions in terms of language, gender or race, civil war, war, class conflict).[11] Such reconciliation may be indicated by an ability of such sectors (including groups and individuals representatives of such sectors) to get along with each other or not, to deal with conflicts humanely and with creativity and civility (Villa-Vicencio 2002:17), or not (e.g. as indicated by a "reconciliation barometer");

- National reconciliation, for example, as understood in South African politics in the 1990s, namely an attempt to address atrocities in the past, to overcome enmities, to build trust and relationships, to develop a shared commitment from most citizens towards the common good in order to be able to live together and work together (see De Gruchy 2002:15);

- Reconciliation between countries or larger groups that can more or less be distinguished geographically and which have been divided by long-standing forms of conflict (if not civil war) and struggles for political independence, for example, in Canada, Ethiopia, Israel, Korea, Northern Ireland, East Timor, the Sudan and the former Yugoslavia to name only a few obvious cases;[12]

- Reconciliation between groups that have little or no contact with each other, but where tensions may nevertheless be prevalent in the form of perceptions, attitudes, jokes and stereotypes, for example, with respect to particular groups of foreigners.

---

10 See Thakatso Mofokeng's comment (in a discussion of Karl Barth's views on reconciliation!): "We can go further and say that the owner and the worker have also been reconciled and equalised. The owner has become the worker as the only appropriate expression of his ownership, while the worker has also become an owner as the only appropriate expression of his being as a worker" (Mofokeng 1986:400).

11 See Nürnberger and Tooke (1988:86).

12 For remarkable case studies of Christian engagement in such forms of reconciliation, see Baum and Wells (1997), also Wink (2005:31-46).

In each case the nature (and closeness) of the previous relationship is important in order to understand what reconciliation would entail in that case. It should be noted that no comment has yet been offered on the nature or quality of such relationships; this would require a more detailed description of particular relationships. Any such a description would be highly complex, since relationships develop over time and are embedded in larger social networks. It is particularly important to note the gendered nature of any such relationship and the role that various forms of power and authority play in structuring and distorting such a relationship.

It should also be noted that this emphasis on relationships precludes a unilateral notion of reconciliation where the victim recovers his or her dignity, is able to bring closure to harmful events of the past through a healing of memories, and is able to narrate the story of his or her life in this light. This may be understood as healing (or as reconciliation with oneself), but not as social reconciliation.

Despite this emphasis on various forms of prior relationships, it should not be assumed that such a relationship existed at all before the need for reconciliation emerged. This is all too often not the case (see below). Moreover, it should also not be assumed that such a prior relationship was ever healthy in the past. In the context of patriarchy, slavery, colonialism and imperialism that is hardly ever the case. The question is therefore what the "re-" in reconciliation might entail (see below). For the moment it would suffice to say that even where healthy prior relationships existed, reconciliation would mean different things, given the different kinds of relationships that existed previously.

These diverse contexts in which the term reconciliation is used does raise the question of whether conceptual clarity is possible at all. The danger is that the term can become a vacuum cleaner that absorbs almost all other concepts and thus becomes meaningless. The logic of interpersonal relationships is quite different from that of the interplay between social groups, population groups or even "cosmic reconciliation". Yet, since the word "reconciliation" is indeed used in all these contexts, it may be necessary to allow for some conceptual fuzziness instead of prematurely narrowing the scope of its usage. This contribution therefore deliberately employs examples of reconciliation from the full range of contexts mentioned above. Again, the aim is not to address any one of the substantive issues, but to gain as much conceptual clarity as may be possible with such an elusive concept.

This emphasis on the nature and quality of relationships may still be misleading as reconciliation takes place within a wider network of relationships that may include a highly complex network of agents or perpetrators (including architects, implementers and collaborators[13]), victims (or better, survivors), affected parties, beneficiaries,[14] inheritors,[15] onlookers, spectators,[16] bystanders, sympathisers, mediators, faraway

---

13 For this helpful distinction, see Swartz & Scott (2012).

14 It has been widely noted that the South African Truth and Reconciliation Commission focused on an extremely narrow agenda, namely the perpetrators and the victims of politically motivated gross violations of human rights. It thus did not address countless other ways in which human dignity was violated during the decades under review. It also did not address the issue of the beneficiaries of structural injustices. In other words, it focused on revolutionary and repressive violence, and not so much on the structural violence that elicited resistance in the first place. See especially Mamdani (1996), Maluleke (1999) and numerous subsequent contributions.

15 Swartz and Scott (2012:16) define inheritors as "those born after the proximal injustice had ended but who experience its consequences, inheriting either the dishonour or the benefit (and in some cases both simultaneously)".

16 See Allan Boesak's reflections entitled "Between Reitz, a rock, and a hard place" in Boesak and DeYoung (2012:93-111). The role of the spectators in this "incident" (as the university management called it) was highly significant. The video made by "the Reitz four" to protest against the integration of university residences was entered in a "cultural competition" and won an award to the "roaring approval of the students who entered the cultural competition". Moreover, the media attention that the case provoked polarised the "spectators". Amidst black anger, expressed by one of the workers as "We feel like toilets", a "disturbingly large section" of the white community responded in angry denial and justification: "they accused blacks of intolerance and racism in reverse; of lacking a sense of humour and festering in unjustified and needless anger; and, worst of all, of the inability to emulate the magnanimity of Mandela" (Boesak & DeYoung 2012:97). This indicates that the event cannot be trivialised as one "incident" of racism by four individuals. It has to be recognised as the symptom of an underlying systemic problem in the university as an institution, a sector of the population and indeed the country as a whole. The word "spectators" should thus not be understood as a euphemism for "onlookers" or innocent "bystanders" but indeed as "supporters".

observers, the dead[17] and future generations (see also Hay 1998:122-127). In traditional communities any conflict between two individuals had to be addressed by the community as a whole, since this affected the social cohesion of the community. Its wellbeing and perhaps even its survival were at stake. Traditionally, the role of the community to bring the perpetrator to justice, to condemn wrongdoing and to shame perpetrators was widely recognised, even though stigma is nowadays recognised to be highly ambiguous. The role of the community is especially crucial in order to provide support for victims/survivors in a variety of ways: to regain dignity and honour, to provide safety for the survivor, to help remember and mourn, to assist with the reconnection with others, to establish solidarity with other victims or survivors:

> Restoration of the breach between the traumatised person and the community depends, first, upon public acknowledgement of the traumatic event and, second, upon some form of community action. Once it is publicly recognized that a person has been harmed, the community must take action to assign responsibility for the harm and repair the injury. These two responses – recognition and restitution – are necessary to rebuild the survivor's sense of order and justice (see Hay 1998:123).

The same need to recognise the wider social network applies to conflict between workers and management, genocide in Rwanda or apartheid in South Africa. It involves a widening circle of others and cannot be restricted to the two parties concerned in the conflict. Reconciliation is embedded in a social environment that is itself embedded in a biophysical environment. The need for reconciliation is indeed nothing but cosmic in scope (see Kistner 1986:80). This raises the question of whether reconciliation between two individuals or small groups would be at all possible in a socio-political environment characterised by oppressive structures and severe inequalities. Allan Boesak observed in 1979 that reconciliation could only be possible when "oppressive

---

17   The challenge that is posed in this regard is articulated in the words of a survivor of the Rwandan genocide: "I don't understand this word 'reconciliation.' I can't reconcile with people, even if they are in prison ... If a person comes to ask my forgiveness, I will pardon him after he has resuscitated the members of my family that he killed" (quoted in Weinstein 2011:8).

structures of economic and political injustice have been torn down; after power, rights and responsibility are no longer the privilege of the happy few, but shared by all" (quoted in Hay 1998:33). At the same time it should be clear that reconciliation at a micro level cannot be determined by social cohesion at a macro level. The transformation of society at a macro level can be stimulated by interactions between individuals and small groups.

The classic Catholic notion of penance introduces an ecclesial dimension at this point. *Lumen Gentium* stressed this communitarian dimension of reconciliation: "Those who approach the sacrament of Penance obtain pardon from the mercy of God for the offence committed against him and are at the same time reconciled with the Church, which they have wounded by their sin, and which by charity, example, and prayer seeks their conversion" (quoted in Hay 1998:77). The whole community works for the conversion of the sinner. This is based on a form of cosmic reconciliation in which in Christ reconciled the world to Godself (2 Cor 5:19). Reconciliation is thus with God, with the church and with those who have been sinned against. In this way the sacrament constituted an ecclesial space in which the gap between reconciliation at a micro and a macro level can be addressed.

Aspects of the dynamics of reconciliation

It is possible to analyse a number of logical aspects of the dynamics of reconciliation with respect to a prior relationship, the first breach of that relationship, ensuing conflict leading to a sense of crisis, intermediate steps to redress the wrongs, and eventually some form of reconciliation that will allow the relationship to flourish again. Such an analysis can help one to identify specific aspects that curtail the possibility of the process of reconciliation in particular cases. It may be helpful to first list these aspects and then investigate some of them in more depth.

It should be noted, though, that this listing should not be confused with a neat and prescribed theological sequence which, as Villa-Vicencio (2002:4) observes, has bedevilled political debate on national conflict.

But at least it can help us to see reconciliation as a process that extends over a period of time and not only as a goal.

- The nature (or closeness) of the *prior relationship*, if any (see above). This will necessarily influence the desirability and structure of some form of reconciliation where appropriate.

- Acts of *wrongdoing* leading to a breach in the prior relationship, involving specific words, specific deeds, sloth, perceptions, attitudes and personality clashes. The breach may be the result of competing self-interests, or may result from deliberate and evil intentions (e.g. crime, rape, murder), or may be more or less accidental (e.g. road accidents, incidents of negligence). Such wrongdoing may be extended over time in the form of oppression, both at an individual and at a societal level, where the perpetrator seeks to exercise power and control over the victim.[18]

- This may result in *structural violence*, namely imbalances, maladjustments and injustices built into the social order as a result of the abuse of power by some groups in pursuing their collective self-interest at the cost of others (see Nürnberger & Tooke 1988:86).

- The possibility of *ensuing conflict* through mutual accusations, with an aggravating and/or mitigating impact on the understanding of the seriousness of the breach in the relationship. This may become extended over time (e.g. marriage conflict, family feuds, civil war). This may well lead to a spiral of conflict involving animosity, mistrust, hatred and revenge.

- The *impact* of such wrongdoing *on the victim(s)*: 1) an assessment by the victim (or on behalf of the victim) of the harm that was done (economic, psychological, medical, social, status in community); 2) the realization of a sense of loss and owning the pain and grief associated with that; 3) the victim's response, which may entail shock, denial, anger (or resentment and frustration), bargaining and acceptance of the harm that

---

18 Hannah Arendt's analysis of Adolf Eichmann is insightful: "The perpetrator's first goal appears to be the enslavement of his victim, and he accomplishes this goal by exercising despotic control over every aspect of the victim's life. But simple compliance rarely satisfies him; he appears to have a psychological need to justify his crimes, and for this he needs the victim's affirmation. Thus he relentlessly demands from his victim professions of respect, gratitude, or even love. His ultimate goal appears to be the creation of a willing victim. Hostages, political prisoners, battered women, and slaves have all remarked upon the captor's curious psychological dependence on his victim" (quoted in Daye 2004:129).

was experienced as irreversible;[19] 4) the related suffering of those affected by such wrongdoing; and 5) the derived suffering of those who show empathy in solidarity with the victims. As Denise Ackermann (1996) suggests, this impact is perhaps best expressed in the form of lament.

- Various *responses to such wrongdoing* by the victim or on behalf of the victim, including passivity, resentment,[20] righteous indignation, wrath and anger over injustices perpetrated,[21] leading to forms of protest and the naming of evil, demanding compensation or retribution, the impulse for satisfaction and punishment commensurate to the harm that was done, the validation of acts of revenge and vindictiveness, but also acts of retaliation in the form of vindictiveness or a blind destructive fury, even a reign of terror (Willa Boesak 1996; De Gruchy 2002:169).

- *Confronting the perpetrator* (or representatives of an institution) with the consequences of his or her actions by naming and articulating the harm that was done. This may be done directly or indirectly through the mechanisms of society or the law. The most important instruments that societies have developed to deal with that are various legal systems (both through civil law and criminal law). This implies the need for the truth to be told, verified in front of witnesses and recognised as such by the victim/ survivor, the perpetrator and other affected parties in order to specify the nature, scope and gravity of the perpetrator's involvement.[22] In this way the perpetrator has to be exposed to the full horror that his (or her) actions

---

19 This follows the famous analysis by Elizabeth Kübler-Ross of five stages of coming to terms with any loss. See also Dorothy Sölle's analysis of the stages of coming to terms with suffering, namely muteness and a lack of comprehension, pain, crying and lament, and then liberation (in Ackermann 1996:54-55).

20 As Russell Daye (following insights from Joseph Butler) observes, wrongdoing entails the implicit statement by the perpetrator to the victim: "I am essentially more important than you are". He adds: "It is acceptable for me to trample your dignity or rights because I am a more important person than you. The generation of resentment within the injured person is a rejection of that claim. It is a counter-assertion of that person's worth" (Daye 2004:14).

21 Boesak comments on the legitimacy of rightful anger: "There is something deeply wrong when we can no longer be outraged by injustice and inhumanity, and it is grossly unfair to act as if that anger is an offense to God or to decent humanity" (in Boesak & DeYoung 2012:107). He adds: "Just as the victim has to hear the words of truth and contrition ... it is necessary for the perpetrator to see and hear the consequences of the wrongful act in order to understand the depth of the forgiveness given" (Boesak & DeYoung 2012:108).

22 Here it is necessary to recognise layered "orders of truth" (a phrase derived from Albie Sachs). Following and building upon Boesak and DeYoung (2012:142-143), I suggest that one can find five such orders of truth, namely scientific facts, forensic truth, personal truth (being known by someone), the truth of "wounded memories", social or inter-subjective truth established through conversation, and

caused and to the revulsion, righteous anger and indignation of the public.[23] However, the judicial system can deal with only a tiny fraction of the hurt and guilt in society. Since not all injustices can be brought to court, there is a need for other processes such as direct confrontation and third-party intervention strategies such as counselling, mediation, story-telling and a retrieval of common memory.[24]

- In this process of confrontation *story-telling and the establishing of common memories* are crucial for the sake of the victim/survivor, for the healing of memories[25] and to avoid cultural amnesia.[26] This may be traumatic, since the will to expose wrongdoing is countered by the victim's inclination to avoid and repress intensely painful memories (Dowdall 1996:34).[27]

---

truth in the form of resilient hope, expressed through an inspiring prophetic vision for the future.

23 Terry Dowdall (1996:33) observes that this is psychologically a necessary process for the perpetrator. Therapy cannot be offered to torturers who are plagued by their past actions without such a public confrontation.

24 Following insights from Richard Niebuhr, Dirkie Smit (1995:4) observes that the role of memory is crucial precisely because we do not always know what we have done – and are still doing to one another. We have no idea of the effect of our actions on others, not even on those who are the closest to us. For example, we do not know as parents, save in fragmentary ways, what we are doing to our children.

25 Charles Villa-Vicencio (1997:31) comments that it is perhaps only by sharing our stories with one another that we can hope to transcend the boundaries of our past and reach towards a shared future. We need to fit partisan memories into a greater story that unites us, since groups tend to tell their stories in a way that serves their collective self-interest. He quotes the following words from James Cone in this regard: "Every people has a story to tell, something to say to themselves, their children, and to the world about how they think and live, as they determine their reason for being ... When people can no longer listen to the other people's stories, they become enclosed within their own social context ... And then they feel they must destroy other people's stories" (quoted in Villa-Vicencio 1997:31). He then recalls words from Ellen Kuzwayo: "We need more stories, never mind how painful the exercise might be. This is how we will learn to love one another. Stories help us to understand, to forgive, and to see things through someone else's eyes" (quoted in Villa-Vicencio 1997:37). Indeed, "there is a wealth of memory and healing power in storytelling".

26 Kistner (1986:90-91) observes a distinction between granting amnesty and amnesia, both of which are derived from the same Greek root. He suggests that the person of the offender may be allowed to become forgotten, but that the impact of the offence should be remembered in order to prevent a repetition of the offence.

27 Daye (2004:127-128), drawing on the work of others, explains the role of memory in overcoming trauma: traumatic memories are not encoded like ordinary adult memories in a linear, narrative fashion that is integrated into

Here the temporality of the process of reconciliation should be respected: shock is a necessary response to trauma in order to protect the victim. Articulation should not take place too soon (in which case the memories of the past would be too difficult to handle), but also not too late (in which case healing cannot take place). It is indeed difficult to bring closure without at least some rudimentary knowledge of the circumstances around the loss that was suffered. Although truth-telling does not necessarily lead to reconciliation, reconciliation without such clarification is hardly possible (Daye 2004:43). For victims and their relatives it is often more important to establish the truth than to exact punishment for the perpetrator (see Wink 2005:30).[28] Remembering the past can be a catalyst to acknowledge the gravity of the offence, to render a denial of the past impossible and to express emotions over trauma in the context of communal respect and support (Hay 1998:130). This also requires the construction of a coherent system of meaning to put the legacy of the past in that perspective. In this way a sense of community and identity can be regained (Hay 1998:131). The memory of the past should not be placed prematurely in a reconciliation straightjacket. Such memories do not necessarily invoke either vengeance or reconciliation; they can also serve a witness and prophetic warning not to underplay structural injustices.[29]

- The *need for the perpetrator to recognise and assess the harm that was done* to the other (or to both parties concerned), to the quality of the prior relationship (if any) and to the possibility of continuing with mutually beneficial interaction within that relationship. In this sense reconciliation entails the need to face and accept unwelcome truths, to reconcile oneself with something, for example, accepting salary cuts instead of retrenchments (Asmal, Asmal & Roberts 1997:46). How is this possible? How can the

---

an ongoing life story. They are instead frozen and wordless. They do not bring forth stories but symptoms. The survivor of traumatic experiences retains them as horrible images that burst out in nightmares and can dominate the person as an *idée fixe*. A major task in healing work is the transformation of these memories into narrative form. This gives the survivor some power over the memories, and it serves as preparation for the incorporation of the traumatic event and its damaging effects into a new self-image and self-understanding. In order to put the painful memories into narrative, however, they have to be verbalized, and this is often resisted both by the victim and by the people around the victim."

28 Wink (2005:30) quotes Sheena Duncan in this regard: "Most of the direct victims of the covert violent attacks and assassinations carried out by the forces of the old apartheid state say that they are ready to forgive, but they must know who it is that they are forgiving for what."

29 Drawing on the analogy of remembering the Holocaust, Grunebaum-Ralph and Stier (1999:148) speaks of "the right not to reconcile: the assertion of the right of the victimised to define both the limits of dialogue and the configurations of the memorial landscape."

perpetrator be brought to such a recognition? As Jürgen Moltmann (2012:182-183) observes, "because perpetrators always have only short memories, they are dependent on the long memories of the victims if they are to arrive at self-knowledge." Would that suffice, though? In structural terms: how do those in positions of political, economic or social power come to the point of recognising the impact of forms of domination on others? Anthony Balcomb (1988:134-137) addresses this question in structural terms that may well have analogues in terms of personal relationships with reference to four possibilities: reconciliation through repression (which entails keeping "peace" through military order), through reform (making gradual concessions in order to avoid a war of attrition), through revolution (by first altering the constellations of power), or through revival (leading to a voluntary relinquishing of power).

- An *assessment of the proportionality of damages and guilt* (see below). One may argue that enmity always has an impact on both parties concerned and on the relationship. However, the damage, pain and suffering are typically not equally distributed. This implies the need to describe and assess the harm that was done. In many cases in complex human relationships both parties have some shared responsibility for what has gone wrong. However, this shared responsibility is again not necessarily an equal responsibility. It requires reflection on the proportionality of guilt. This becomes a complex task because of disputes over the origin of conflict, provocation, aggravating circumstances and retaliation. In such cases the process of reconciliation can only proceed if both parties concerned are in principle willing to suspend judgement over the guilt of the other and are open to see guilt on their own side. Here some form of third-party intervention or intermediaries would typically be necessary.

- The *expectation* and *anticipation* of the victim as to what form of reparation would be needed in order to give back what can be given back or, alternatively, what form of compensation would be commensurate with the harm that was done. This is, of course, related to an assessment by the victim of the harm that was done. The expectation of the victim may be realistic, generous or exaggerated. Such expectations may well be expressed in the form of claims through the instruments of civil law. Since the perpetrator may or may not agree with such an assessment and estimation, third-party invention is often required. Although forgiveness (unlike amnesty) can only be offered unconditionally, this does not exclude the role of such anticipation. Here clarity is required as to what it is that is forgiven (see the discussion on reparation, compensation and restitution below).

- The need for *the perpetrator to acknowledge some form of involvement in the violation of the rights of the victim*/survivor and to offer an account of that involvement. Alternatively, the perpetrator may, perhaps in order to save face (not to be shamed in public[30]) or to avoid the consequences of such wrongdoing, argue that his or her acts were not blameworthy – by denying that this was done intentionally, or by indicating that this was done accidentally, or by maintaining that this is what anyone else would have done under such circumstances. Another option may be to argue that such wrongdoing was done under provocation, that it was a form of revenge, or that the other is at least partly to be blamed (which would prompt further reflection on the proportionality of guilt). The perpetrator may therefore engage in self-defence, legitimising his or her actions, respond with further accusations, scapegoat others for the harm that was done, plead innocence, or claim to be unaware of the consequences of his or her actions. This may lead to a lengthy process of mutual accusations and aggravating actions that will cause even more harm to the prior relationship. As Kader Asmal and his co-authors noted, reconciliation requires "an ending of the divisive cycle of accusation, denial and counter-accusation; not a forgetting of these accusations and counter-accusations, but more a settling of them through a process of evaluation – like the accountant's job of reconciling conflicting claims before closing a ledger book" (Asmal, Asmal & Roberts 1997:47).

- A sense of *regret*. The perpetrator may also come to an awareness of the negative consequences of past actions for himself or herself. This may include fear of punishment or revenge, a realisation of the psychological impact of such wrongdoing on the perpetrator (in terms of a guilty conscience, coping with feelings of guilt, living with memories of trauma, nightmares, etc.), and the recognition of the loss of a relationship. Alternatively, the perpetrator may of course also show no or little regret for the harm done to the victim. Again, this may be defended on the basis of righteous anger, revenge or a refusal to accept moral responsibility for the harm that was done.

- An internal process whereby *the perpetrator comes to accept responsibility for wrongdoing* or at least his or her share in the wrongdoing. This may result

---

30 The role of shame should not be underestimated, especially in traditional societies. Experiencing shame by the perpetrator may be beneficial in order to express regret and remorse. However, the danger of "toxic shame" should also be recognised, i.e. "shame that leads to a denial of truth and reality and therefore shame that is potentially destructive" (De Gruchy 2002:190). Shame may also be a way in which societies express aversion to the acts of the perpetrator, to exert pressure ("shame on you!"), to impose punishment and to uphold moral standards. However, such forms of shaming can easily degenerate into stigmatisation.

from a recognition of the harm done to the perpetrator (who may then wish to get on with his or her life again), the emergence of sympathy for the victim, or through third-party intervention. This may also be the result of a sense of conscience (literally "joint knowledge") or a religious recognition of having sinned before God and against others (see below).

- This sense of responsibility may be experienced in the form of *regret* (in the sense of recognising the impact of wrongdoing and the wrongness of one's prior actions – see above), *resentment* (to acknowledge that past behaviour, attitudes and perceptions were inappropriate and to repudiate such behaviour, attitudes and perceptions in the future), *restraint* (sensing the need to refrain from further accusations even where these may be quite legitimate as a result of the proportionality of guilt), *remorse* (accepting guilt and the impact of the wrongdoing on oneself as the wrongdoer as well as the impact on the victim and also the impact on bystanders and the rest of society), *contrition* (being crushed in spirit by a sense of guilt and shame[31]), *repentance* (recognising the need for moral transformation[32]) and *penitence* (being willing to start a process that may lead to the healing of the prior relationship).[33] Together these aspects may be described in the language of "conversion", an internal process entailing a radical change of heart and mind (*metanoia*), an aversion to former ways of thinking and behaving, leading to different perceptions, attitudes, words and deeds.

---

31 Everett observes that the South African TRC invoked confession (of the truth, if not of guilt), absolution (amnesty) and penance (government reparation). However, no remorse or contrition could be built into the process. He suggests that churches should "try to foster some personal sense of contrition, without which forgiveness will not bring about reconciliation. Moreover, without contrition there is probably little motivation for personal acts of reparation" (Everett 1999:158).

32 Some theologians would argue that repentance is not a condition for forgiveness but the consequence of a recognition of God's forgiveness. Forgiveness precedes repentance. It cannot be conditional; it is either offered freely or not at all. The only sin that is recognised is also recognised to be forgiven. We do not see the problem until we are grasped by the solution (Smit 1995:7). Hay (1998:91) concurs that it is God's forgiveness already given that makes penitence possible. Penitence is what happens to us when we are touched and take up by God's pardon.

33 The Catholic notion of penance includes the aspects of conversion, repentance and "doing penance", to change the direction of one's course of action in order to "re-establish the balance and harmony broken by sin" (Hay 1998:86). Given the ritual of penance, it is often regarded as something private and confidential. By contrast, the public dimensions of reparation are also addressed in this contribution.

Ernst M. Conradie

- This internal process will typically be expressed by showing visible *signs of remorse* (with or without forms of compensation): This may or may not be sincere, depending on whether such remorse is motivated by the perpetrator's concern for the impact of the deeds on him/herself, on the victim or on society. Such remorse is crucial for healing to take place – for both the victim/survivor and the perpetrator.

- In this process the *response by the public in audience,* including the role of the media, should not be underestimated. This may include an expression of sympathy for the victim, a willingness to listen to the stories of both the victims and the perpetrators, acts of solidarity to address the needs of the victim, moral indignation over the acts of the perpetrator, shaming (or stigmatising) the person of the perpetrator, scapegoating or disassociating from the perpetrator. However, if it takes a village to raise a child, the shared culpability[34] of a sector of the public should also be reckoned with.[35] It is society that therefore has to carry the burden for punishing the offender (i.e. at least through paying taxes for correctional services). On this basis, media attention to gross violations of human rights may be warranted, even if this is often sensationalist. The trial of an offender is in a way a trial of the larger society.

- *Acts of reparation* and *compensation.* Following such an internal process of conversion, the perpetrator would want to give back to the victim what can be given back (e.g. in the case of theft), offer (monetary) compensation for reversible damages, render services where appropriate for the sake of rehabilitation, or engage in a redress of wrongs, where possible. In this way the perpetrator will address the most obvious stumbling blocks to reconciliation (e.g. by giving back what can be given back), whether instructed by a confessor or not. However, this is often not possible, for example, in cases of broken goods, when something was used up in the

34 In a class discussion at UWC following a notorious incident when a reckless taxi driver crossed a railway line despite an oncoming train, leading to the death of 10 children (mostly from lower-middle-class families) whom he was transporting from school, the following question was raised: who is the perpetrator and who is the victim? The class was in agreement that everyone who disobeys traffic rules (speeding, jumping traffic lights, not stopping at stop signs, etc.) is to be blamed, since this yields a society where individuals may become reckless to this extent. Such reckless individuals are not exceptions to the rule, but only the worst examples. Blaming the taxi driver and being concerned for the victims would therefore be legitimate, but would not yet address the underlying problem.

35 As Wolfram Kistner (1996:90) observes, "The society and the religious or ideological community or cultural group which has contributed towards shaping the offender shares in the responsibility of the offence and is in need of repentance on its part and forgiveness on the part of God and the victims with the view to facilitating a process of healing and taking precaution against a repetition of the offence." For a discussion, see also Botman (1999).

interim, in cases of permanent bodily harm, lasting psychological damage (e.g. rape) or death (e.g. through murder, accidents or negligence by medical practitioners). Societies therefore need to find innovative ways of dealing with past grievances through punishment (if only to command public respect for the dignity of victims), compensation, satisfaction (doing enough in terms of what can be done) or support for the victims (see the discussion on restitution below).[36] However, when the task of reparation is left to the third parties such as the government to attend to, this may well create confusing allegiances.

- A *confirmation* from the side of the victim/survivor that the reparation or compensation that was received is indeed satisfactory (or not).

- A *confession of guilt* (verbally or in writing) by the perpetrator to the victim/survivor. The perpetrator admits to being responsible for the wrong done and to moral indebtedness to the victim. As Russell Daye observes, the guilty party often offers excuses or explanations alongside the admission of guilt. However, "in the cleanest and best examples of the drama of forgiveness these qualifiers are abandoned and the party in the wrong stands 'naked' before the narrative of its unjust action and asks for forgiveness" (Daye 2004:8). A confession of guilt may, of course, be offered without the process described above. Confessions can be faked, superficial, evoked under pressure,[37] be made for selfish reasons to avoid unwanted consequences, or to elicit a kind of psychological release (since unconfessed guilt may be deemed to cause depression[38]). To say

---

36 The role of acts of reparation is placed here deliberately before a confession of guilt. This does not imply a necessary logic, since this may also follow afterwards. However, the sincerity of any confession of guilt is dependent upon reparation: what can be given back should be given back (or at least promised) even before confessing guilt. The proposed logic here is based on a somewhat tenuous but necessary distinction between acts of reparation (and/or compensation) and acts of restitution (see below).

37 David Bosch (1986:168) observes that "confession of guilt and repentance cannot be imposed by others but is a gift of the Holy Spirit". He adds that the reason why Afrikaner Christians have been so slow to confess their guilt may well be because others have tried so frequently to bludgeon them into do so.

38 As Dietrich Bonhoeffer recognised, open confession is good for the soul, it liberates those in all-too-pious Christian communities from attempts to hide their sins from one another. Confession allows people to be who they are: forgiven sinners before God. Bonhoeffer's (1996:108-110) description of the self-deception of the pious community remains classic: "For the pious community permits no one to be a sinner. Hence all have to conceal their sins from themselves and from the community. We are not allowed to be sinners. Many Christians would be unimaginably horrified if a real sinner were suddenly to turn up among the pious. So we remain alone with our sin, tapped in lies and hypocrisy, for we are in fact sinners." He then emphasises the breakthrough to community through

"Sorry!" does not mean that you are sorry! A mark of true confession is its specificity. It is an exercise in name-giving, as Karl Barth also emphasised. If so, the confession of guilt is accompanied by anticipated shame – which offers an indication of the sincerity of the confession. Guilt and remorse are inner, private emotions, but shame is necessarily public (Boesak & DeYoung 2012:38).

- Such a confession of guilt may be coupled with asking for *forgiveness*. Alternatively (typically without a confession of guilt), one may offer an *apology*, seek *condonation*, request *amnesty* or *remission*, or find *absolution*. These options are clearly not the same. To ask for *forgiveness* with sincerity may be regarded as an indication of the desire of the perpetrator to continue with and restore a healthy relationship with the victim and with the community/society within which both are situated. It is born from the recognition that not all the harm done by the perpetrator can be undone (see the discussion on the "deficit" below). The relationship can therefore only be restored through the victim's forgiveness, signalling the reciprocal desire from the victim to restore this relationship. An *apology* may be offered either on the basis of self-justification by the perpetrator (thus indicating an unwillingness to accept full moral responsibility for the harm done), or on the basis of the assumption that the harm that was done is relatively negligible (for example, bumping into a stranger on the sidewalk, accepting responsibility for not contributing to a common task, indicating that an action was merely insensitive), or that the harm done has to be assessed in terms of mitigating circumstances. A confession of guilt therefore renders the one who confesses more vulnerable than in the case of offering an apology.[39] Seeking *condonation* assumes a denial that an action has caused someone else serious harm. Any little harm can therefore be regarded as negligible. There is actually nothing to forgive. The actions may be condoned. Alternatively, an action may be condoned if it was provoked, done in self-defence or responding to circumstances

---

the practice of confession of sins: "Sin that has been spoken and confessed has lost all of its power. It has been revealed and judged as sin. It can no longer tear apart the community. ... The sinner has been relieved of sin's burden. Now the sinner stands in the community of sinners who live by the grace of God in the cross of Jesus Christ."

39   See the discussion on the place of apology in Wink (2005:46-51). Wink notes the relatively recent phenomenon in statecraft where offering an apology has been extended from one person to another to include apologies from one institution to another and from one country to another. He defines an apology as "a statement of regret that attempts to elicit an act of forgiveness" and adds that it is "a strategic move which attempt to absolve the injuring party of further culpability" (2005:48). Such apologies are often offered long after the event by those who did not commit the crime to descendants of the victims who cannot offer forgiveness either.

beyond one' locus of control. Again such condonation would imply that there is little to forgive. Seeking *amnesty* is similar to asking for forgiveness in that the victim (or society on behalf of the victim) is asked to refrain from pursuing retaliation or punishing the perpetrator. Seeking amnesty, however, is one-sided in that it asks for blanket impunity for the perpetrator and does not imply the need for some form of reconciliation between the perpetrator and the victim. The protection of those who committed gross violations of human rights through their being granted amnesty in the context of the South African TRC is, of course, related to the political settlement reached in the transition to democracy, but cannot prevent perceptions that evil has been condoned in the process. *Remission* may be understood as the shortening of a convict's prison sentence or a refraining from exacting (full) debt, venting one's anger, inflicting punishment or executing a sentence. The full impact of the consequences of the perpetrator's actions for the perpetrator are therefore reduced but not completely annulled. Seeking *absolution* is similar to amnesty in the sense that the perpetrator hopes that punishment for crimes committed will be deferred. Moreover, through absolution the perpetrator is pronounced to be free from blame or further obligation. In a religious context it also includes the forgiveness of sins against God.

- *Contemplation of offering forgiveness* by the victim: weighing up the harm that was done, the deficit that can never be undone (see below), the importance of a continued relationship with the perpetrator, the desirability of social harmony and the victim/survivor's own need to get on with life. Such contemplation implies the consideration of alternative options to fear, resentment, vengeance or retaliation (Daye 2004:17). A crucial but controversial aspect here is the emergence of empathy for the humanity of the enemy, typically in terms of the wisdom to recognise that liberation for the victim depends at least partially upon the liberation of the oppressor. Healing can only take place on the basis of rediscovering the common humanity of all parties concerned. If such forgiveness is offered at all, it has to be offered voluntarily by the victim; it cannot be induced, expected, enforced[40] or demanded on the basis of penitence or acts reparation. Offering forgiveness may be motivated by a conflicting variety of considerations (see below) and requires (psychological) preparation before the victim/survivor can reach the point of offering forgiveness (Daye 2004:16). The nature of the "forgiveness" that may be offered depends on such considerations (leading to condoning a

---

40 Boesak and DeYoung (2012:107) mention the comment from a young woman who testified before the Amnesty Commission of the TRC and found that she was expected not to show her anger at what was done to her: "The oppression was bad … [but] what is much worse, what makes me even angrier, is that they are trying to dictate my forgiveness."

crime, amnesty, compensation, closure for the victim, social harmony, or reconciliation in a restored relationship that can flourish again on the basis of such forgiveness).

- *Offering forgiveness.* Since forgiveness is necessarily a two-way process, it can only take place when it is offered. This raises the question of whether forgiveness is a performative utterance, a process, a transaction, an internal state of mind, or an attitude (see Daye 2004:3). Offering forgiveness comes at a price, namely the willingness of the victim to bear the suffering associated with the harm that was done for the sake of the relationship. It may elicit repentance, but is not necessarily conditional upon repentance or reparation. However, it should be noted that reconciliation is impossible without both forgiveness and repentance.[41]

- *Acceptance that the forgiveness that was offered is genuine* and will therefore not lead to acts of retribution so that the perpetrator is not vulnerable to the victim's vengeance. A more difficult aspect is the "forswearing of resentment" (as the 18th-century bishop Joseph Butler defined forgiveness). It is difficult for the perpetrator to judge whether the victim has forsworn such resentment. For the victim this is equally difficult given the role of recurring memories. Moreover, as Fraser Watts observes, the problem is not only one of offering forgiveness, but also of receiving such forgiveness. This is related to low self-esteem and the defensiveness associated with that. However, it may also involve "a humiliating acknowledgement that one is in the wrong and morally indebted to others" (Watts 2004:59). The problem is not only feelings of guilt or actual guilt, but the sense of shame that the perpetrator experiences. This is more difficult to assuage and makes it difficult for offenders to receive the help they need.

- *The perpetrator's need to respond to the lasting deficit,* namely the forms of harm that cannot be undone through reparation, compensation (see above) or restitution (given the circumstances of the particular case). Again, the victim may have certain expectations as to how the perpetrator should address this deficit so that the relationship can in future be characterised by some rough equity, mutuality and reciprocity. Note that offering forgiveness therefore does not exclude such expectations, even if it can only be offered unconditionally. Forgiveness aimed at reconciliation is offered in anticipation of reciprocity. The forgiven perpetrator thus still

---

41   Vincent Brümmer (2005:43) notes that, "Although I cannot force you to repudiate, I can do my best to persuade you freely to do so. If I were to forgive you without desiring your repentance and urging you to have a change of heart, my forgiveness would merely confirm you in the role as my abuser and myself in the role as your victim. My forgiveness expresses my desire to be reconciled with you despite what you have done to me and not my acquiescence in your continuing to do so and thus to continue to undermine our fellowship. Such acquiescence would leave everything as it is and cannot lead to reconciliation."

owes the victim a response. This response may include the perpetrator's willingness to accept appropriate punishment, some form of restitution, an appropriate gift that is commensurate with the lasting deficit and the ability of the perpetrator to offer something to the victim, making or bringing sacrifices, or a willingness on the side of perpetrator to assist the victim (or the victim's relatives) through offering help, making time and energy available, etc. The agenda for the perpetrator here is one of satisfaction, of doing enough to heal a broken relationship and recognising, through the eyes of the victim, when enough is enough.[42] The response from the perpetrator anticipated by the victim may well disappoint the victim. In that case the willingness of the victim to bear the suffering associated with the harm that was done for the sake of restoring the relationship is not appreciated by the perpetrator. Insult is added to injury. On the other hand, the expectations of the victim may, of course, also be unrealistic. Either way, the possibility of reconciliation will be thwarted.

- *An indication* by the victim *that such forms of restitution are indeed satisfactory*: the perpetrator has suffered enough or has done what could be expected. The remaining deficit can therefore be overlooked, condoned or forgiven.[43]

- A *reciprocal response* from the victim, namely by offering some gift to the perpetrator in order to indicate a desire to continue with a relationship characterised by mutuality and reciprocity.

---

42 Brümmer (2005:76) observes that in relationships based on rights and obligations, the only alternative to satisfaction is punishment (retributive justice) or condonation (in cases where the harm that was done was relatively trivial). One may add the possibility of reparation (giving back what can be given back), compensation and also amnesty (in cases where the harm that was done is not trivial). Where this is not possible (given the lasting deficit) other options need to be found. Brümmer emphasises the need for forgiveness to restore fellowship, because he wishes to maintain that our relationship with God is not merely one based on rights and obligations. However, in my opinion forgiveness can also be used for less intimate relationships.

43 Nürnberger (1989:13) notes that full restitution is in many cases no longer possible. He comments that it is important that restitution is not demanded on a scale that would jeopardise the life chances of the perpetrator. This may lead to further conflict. In some cases, "full restitution would harm society to such an extent that it is in the interest even of the wronged party to make a fresh start and bury the past". Nürnberger adds that cheap reconciliation may then be understood as inadequate forms of restitution. It is cheap for the party which committed the wrong. Reconciliation requires reciprocity, while justice requires that the sacrifices and suffering necessary for reconciliation be distributed as fairly as possible.

- The *willingness* of the perpetrator *to receive and accept such gifts* from the victim and thus to be further indebted.[44] The willingness to receive gifts from one another suggests a willingness to form an equal relationship and may elicit a long process of reciprocal giving and receiving.

- *Experiences of reconciliation* and fellowship that would include joy, gratitude, mutuality, vulnerability, respect for the other, experiencing the relationship as fruitful and mutual flourishing – depending on the nature and intimacy of the prior relationship or new relationships that may have emerged.[45] Reconciliation here means being able to continue with a relationship without the negative impact of that which caused the breach.[46]

- It is also possible to speak of reconciliation in structural terms with respect to larger sectors of a society that have been in conflict with each other as a result of the abuse of power, resulting in structural violence in the social order. Here reconciliation requires an acknowledgement of the abuse of power, an agreement to cooperate in addressing the structural imbalances by instituting social mechanisms that balance out power and privilege, to tolerate differences of race, culture and creed, and banning discrimination on such grounds.[47]

---

44 As John Macmurray observed, "If in my relation to you I insist on behaving generously toward you and refuse to accept your generosity in return, I make myself the giver and you the recipient. This is unjust to you. I put you in my debt and refuse to let you repay the debt. In that case I make the relation an unequal one. You are to have continual cause to be grateful to me, but I am not to be grateful to you. This is the worst kind of tyranny and is shockingly unfair to you" (quoted in Brümmer 2005:39). It destroys the possibility of mutuality.

45 See also Miroslav Volf's perceptive analysis of the four movements in the drama of embrace: opening the arms, waiting, closing the arms and opening them again (Volf 1996:140-147).

46 Klaus Nürnberger (1989:12) offers a helpful definition of reconciliation in its most basic form: "Reconciliation means that fellowship is restored between two parties after a conflict has been resolved. A conflict is resolved when the guilty party repents of its mistakes [wrongdoing] and tries to rectify the situation as far as possible, while the other party is willing to forgive and suffer whatever can no longer be rectified. Because both repentance and forgiveness are sacrificial acts, reconciliation is never possible without suffering." Nürnberger adds that reconciliation presupposes restitution through which the wronged party is compensated for its losses. See also the NIR's definition of reconciliation: "Reconciliation is the agreement between two parties in conflict to forgive and accept each other. This presupposes that both parties are committed to remove the causes of the conflict as far as they can be removed, and bear them as far as they cannot be removed" (in Nürnberger & Tooke 1988:84).

47 See the NIR's theological statement on reconciliation in Nürnberger and Tooke (1988:86).

- If such *reconciliation might not come to fruition,* one may still identify degrees of being able to get on with the rest of one's life and of getting along with each other, i.e. relationships that are not characterised by hatred, the desire for revenge, vengeance, insults, assaults and further gross violations of human rights. Indeed, reconciliation understood as a relationship characterised by equity, reciprocity and mutual respect (not necessarily the intimacy of fellowship) may often prove to be an elusive, almost eschatological dream. In such cases one may identify a range of strategies that may have to suffice: staying out of one another's way, tolerance, more or less peaceful coexistence, finding a space to deal with past grievances, reaching some form of compromise, being able to cooperate, showing some respect for one another's rights, the emergence of sympathy and respect, getting along for better or for worse, and the emergence of relationships characterised by mutuality, sharing and reciprocity.[48] Although one may also adopt a more qualitative definition of "radical reconciliation" (see Boesak & DeYoung 2012),[49] distinguishing it for example from conflict resolution (see Baum & Wells 1997:189), an approach is adopted here to speak of degrees of reconciliation so that the secular usage of the term may also be acknowledged. The emphasis on degrees of reconciliation and on reconciliation as a process is therefore not aimed at lowering the bar, but to recognise the full complexity of the process and to avoid attempts to sidestep the pain that this entails. Indeed, as Miroslav Volf (1996:109) observes, the question is not how we accomplish some final reconciliation (that may be left in God's hands), but what resources we need to live in peace in the absence of such final reconciliation.

One may group these aspects of the process of reconciliation together under aspects that focus on the past, its impact on the present, and creating a new future (see, for example, Hay 1998:129-135). It is important to add a reminder here that these aspects of the process

---

48 As Villa-Vicencio (2002:4) observes, "the goal of reconciliation is the transcendence of an impasse that has the capacity to destroy." However, being able to get on with one's own life "does not necessarily mean becoming friends with the person responsible for one's suffering, nor does it mean forgiving that person. Very few accomplish this. Perhaps most people can only deal with their past suffering intermittently" (2002:8). Such an ability to get on with one's own life is best not equated with reconciliation, unless understood as reconciliation with oneself.

49 Boesak and DeYoung (2012:155) rightly challenge the "modest" notion of reconciliation propagated by Villa-Vicencio and others as a dangerous modesty that is deleterious for the poor and powerless. It may easily amount to a plea for modesty instead of justice.

of reconciliation should not be understood in a linear way or even as necessary in all cases. Although a certain logic may be described, this does not suggest a sequence or phases of a process. Often the reality is far more complex. Reconciliation as an outcome of this process requires something constituting an art, an imaginative way of responding to dehumanising conflict.[50]

Another important reminder is that reconciliation does not necessarily imply the intimacy associated with the experiences of reconciliation and fellowship mentioned above. One can also speak about reconciliation between companies, rival sports clubs or countries. Intimate fellowship would not be the appropriate term to describe whatever reconciliation between a rapist and a rape survivor previously not known to him might entail!

On the basis of an identification of these aspects involved in the process of arriving at reconciliation, it may be helpful to investigate some of these aspects in more depth.

Reparation and the notion of a deficit

Any act of wrongdoing between individuals or groups implies a "deficit" that can never be undone. For example, if in a moment of negligence I bumped into your brand new car, you would probably be very angry, especially if you were in a hurry to get to an important meeting. There is nothing that I could ever do to nullify the trouble that I caused you. I (my insurance) could pay for the damage to your car, but the time lost and the frustration caused cannot be repaid. The deficit is therefore partly a function of the transitoriness of our lives. There will always remain a deficit, even if I express remorse, accept responsibility and offer you a nice gift to acknowledge my indebtedness to you. The gift should not be insignificant in order to acknowledge the magnitude of the deficit. It should not be excessive either, since that may be taken as a bribe and would in turn make you indebted to me. If we happen to be neighbours and sit together on the committee of a community organisation, you

---

50   As Njabulo Ndebele notes, it has to do with "who we can become" (quoted in Villa-Vicencio 2002:17).

may later be willing to offer me a word of forgiveness to indicate that our continued relationship is more important to you than the harm that I have caused you. If I accept that your forgiveness is sincere, we may shake hands, drink a beer together and laugh about the matter in years to come.

The deficit is in the above example relatively small. Reparation can cover almost all the damage. Consider how the deficit increases exponentially in the following examples: a) If I bumped into your child through negligent, reckless or drunken driving; b) If your child is subsequently hospitalised for three months but recovers fully (my insurance can pay for the hospital costs, but cannot undo the pain and trauma caused to you or to the child); c) if your child is subsequently paralysed; d) if your child died as a result of this "accident"; e) if I did that deliberately to spite you; f) if I raped and killed your child. Note the differences in the deficit in cases of contractual law, civil law and criminal law. Note also that, although the term "deficit" is derived from the world of finance; it is used here by metaphoric extension precisely to indicate something that cannot be counted and therefore cannot be compensated in financial terms.

Another example of this deficit may be found in a socio-political context. Consider someone whose house was taken away through the implementation of the Group Areas Act in the 1960s. This person may have received compensation for the house (if it has been demolished) or may even have received the same house back some 30 years later. That would be cause for much joy and celebration. However, there remains a severe deficit: such reparation cannot undo the misery of living for 30 years with the impact of such a forced removal. Indeed, nothing can undo that, if the best years of one's life have been ruined through such injustice.

In the context of long-lasting conflicts between groups, this notion of a deficit becomes far more entangled. The economic, social and educational impact of centuries of imperialism, slavery, colonialism and apartheid in South Africa created an immense deficit. Two decades after the transition to a democratic dispensation this deficit is undoubtedly still felt by many "previously disadvantaged" citizens, often with considerable resentment and anger. However, this deficit will necessarily become more and more entangled with subsequent history, subsequent generations, black empowerment, affirmative action and the new constellations of inequalities that have been emerging. The impact of temporality should again be noted here: the longer it takes to address such structural inequalities, the more difficult it will become.

A crucial difference between reparation and dealing with this deficit has to be noted. Reparation may be understood as addressing the harm that can indeed be undone. Only when that is done can the deficit be addressed. Only on that basis is reconciliation possible. Consider a simple example: if I have stolen my friend's textbook to study for the exam, she would obviously be upset if this is discovered. No reconciliation can be expected if I do not return the textbook. Only then can the deficit be addressed, namely her lack of opportunity to study and subsequent failure in the exam. What can be given back should be given back. Reparation is the minimum standard of justice, but it does not suffice for reconciliation. Reparation can never compensate for the experience of loss, suffering and humiliation of the victim (Boesak & DeYoung 2012:138).

In a famous parable, told at a TRC public meeting, Rev. Mxolisi Mpambani explained what is at stake in reparation:

> There were two boys living opposite each other. John stole a bicycle from Tom and then after a year John came to Tom and said: "Tom, I stole your bicycle and what I now need is reconciliation." Then Tom looked at John and said: "Where is my bicycle?" He said: "No, I am not talking about your bicycle now, I am talking about reconciliation." (quoted in Du Toit 1998:117).

It should be obvious, though, that there are many cases where injustices cannot be undone through acts of reparation. Consider the following cases: where one child has taken another's apple and eaten it; where I borrowed your new bicycle and had an accident with it (even if the damage is repaired, it will no longer be or feel "new"); where I cannot repay a loan as a result of bankruptcy; where something cannot be undone in principle because of the nature of a crime (spreading gossip, insults, maiming for life as a result of assault, rape, murder); where the long-term damage to a culture is irreversible (as a consequence of imperialism); and where financial damage can no longer be calculated (as a result of colonisation, systemic oppression). In each of these cases some form of reparation may be possible. However, the deficit will be much greater than in cases where the impact of the material damage can be undone.

Reparation may include forms of compensation. If, in the example above, the bicycle was damaged irreparably, I cannot return that bicycle, but I may be able to buy you a similar one. If you were hospitalised for two months as a result of my negligent driving, I cannot undo that, but I (or my insurance) can compensate you for loss of income. If your child is paralysed as a result of my negligent driving, I would also have to compensate your family for a lifetime of medical costs, the loss of opportunity and for the pain and trauma that I caused. Such compensation is, of course, the subject matter of civil law. However, if I am bankrupt and have no insurance, such compensation will not be commensurable with the damage caused. This is then added to whatever deficit there will be, irrespective of any form of compensation. It should be noted that the distinction between reparation, compensation and restitution (see the discussion below) that is made here is not widely employed in the literature in the field of jurisprudence. Often restitution is understood to include reparation and compensation. Accordingly, restitution is an act of restoration that seeks to rectify a case of unjust enrichment at the expense of another by giving something back to the victim. Such restitution could include goods that are returned, money that is transferred, but also services rendered by the perpetrator to the victim or the victim's relatives or community. However, given the distinction between reparation, compensation and restitution that is made here, such services rendered may best be regarded as a form of restitution.

This analysis may have interesting implications for the debt that we owe to God according to covenantal theology. The need for sacrifices is born from a recognition that such deficits owed to God cannot be paid back. Reconciliation between God and humanity is only possible if the deficit is written off, if it is forgiven by God. Through rituals of sacrifice one offers part of the whole deficit to acknowledge this deficit, in the hope that this would be seen as symbolic of the whole, or to express gratitude for the forgiveness that was granted. Of course, it may easily be taken for granted that such an offering would indeed suffice for the whole. That would be insulting to God, as if God can be bribed. What would be worse is if the damage than can be undone through reparation has not been addressed yet. It would simply not do to arrive at the altar to make peace with God, if one has not yet done what could be done to resolve the conflict with one's brother or sister (Matt 5:23-24). That may be why the prophets would insist that what God demands is justice (reparation), not rituals of sacrifice that are aimed at addressing the deficit (Micah 6:6-8). Only once reparation and compensation have been addressed, as far as this is possible, can the deficit be ritually addressed.

The proportionality of guilt

There are times when it would be appropriate to recognise the proportionality of guilt and other times when it would not be appropriate. In the discussion below the need for discernment in this regard will become evident. As a general rule it would be appropriate to raise the issue of proportionality of guilt when there is indeed guilt on both sides, but when any suggestion of an equality of guilt needs to be resisted (e.g. in cases of structural violence and revolutionary violence). It would not be appropriate when a clear distinction between victim and perpetrator is possible or where guilt is roughly equally proportioned. Let us explore these in inverse order.

A breach in an intimate relationship can seldom be blamed on one of the parties alone. Consider broken marriages or young adults who have become estranged from their families. These situations may involve an intricate web of relationships, role responsibilities, gender stereotypes and so forth within an extended family. In such contexts it may be pastorally inappropriate to apportion blame and to speak about the proportionality of guilt. It is more appropriate to find a way out of the reality of a broken relationship. At the same time it would not be possible to heal the relationship without due consideration of the specific incidents that may have contributed to the breach in the relationship. However, this may open a proverbial can of worms, leading to endless recriminations. If someone approaches a broken relationship from a position of moral righteousness, apportioning blame and claiming innocence, this is bound to raise objections (De Gruchy 2002:192). At some point it may therefore be better to simply accept shared guilt and to focus on the worth of the relationship. Forgiveness would only be possible if continuing with a relatively close relationship is considered by all the parties concerned to be more important than the harm that was experienced within that relationship. At this point one may find phrases such as "we are all equally guilty before God" or "no one sin is greater than another" helpful to avoid a callous calculation of who is to be blamed more than the other.

Nevertheless, a pastoral over-eagerness to restore such a relationship may ignore systemic forms of inequality in a prior relationship. This is especially true of gendered relationships, but may apply to any form of differentiation in power in terms of race, class, caste, age or rank. The underlying problem is that a rough equality in mutual guilt can easily be abused by a dominant party to blame the victim/survivor for the suffering experienced. If such guilt is internalised by the victim, this can cause severe psychological trauma and is easily abused to further entrench forms of domination. One notorious example is the way rape victims are blamed for what happened to them (e.g. "What did she wear that night?"). Other examples come from forms of domestic violence such as wife battering. Consider also the way parents blame themselves for the ways their teenage children sometimes abuse them.

One may also mention the way "state theology" was directed against the violent resistance to the repressive violence of the apartheid state as the primary cause for social unrest. Can one equate violence used in the struggle for liberation with structural or repressive violence? The worst cases may be the way offences by prisoners are criminalised in concentration camps, but one may find similar examples in South African society, which is characterised by systemic economic inequalities.[51] In all cases where gross violations of human rights occurred, it is therefore necessary to distinguish carefully between the perpetrator and the victim. The perpetrator may be regarded as a victim too, but a proper understanding of his or her guilt has to be based on the underlying dynamics and historic constellations of power in each situation.[52] To even raise the notion of the proportionality of guilt in such a context would be to take sides against the victim/survivor (see Boesak & DeYoung 2012:105).

On the other hand, one might also argue that an emphasis on the proportionality of guilt is precisely what is required in such a context. The South African Truth and Reconciliation Commission investigated any politically motivated gross violations of human rights, including those associated with the armed struggle and abuses in military camps of liberation movements. One may indeed identify perpetrators of gross violations of human rights on all sides. However, the structural violence associated with apartheid, violent resistance against that and the violent repression of such resistance cannot be equated.[53] That is why the proportionality of guilt has to be recognised and addressed.

---

51 In his discussion of the Reitz event, Boesak offers a telling illustration of the dynamics of power conveyed in a single word. The term "squeeza" is apparently used by white students for female domestic workers (also in university residences), whereas black students use the word "Mama". Boesak comments: "The very word conjures up disturbing historical images and associations of subservience and domination, of power and powerlessness; a relentless hand squeezing out every drop of submission, draining the overpowered of will and dignity" (Boesak & DeYoung 2012:104). Moreover, this may still hide sexual repression: the squeezing is not done by hand alone.

52 Boesak comments: "The abuser will begin to find redemption when he sees himself through the eyes of his victim" (in Boesak & DeYoung 2012:107).

53 This raises the classic question of whether reactionary violence may be condoned, for example, as a form of self-defence or in the form of the "just war" theory. In the context of a discussion of the proportionality of guilt, the words of a wise pastor may be more appropriate: "There is no verse in the Bible that suggests that my sins will be forgiven simply because others have sinned more gravely than I did."

Moreover, a clear line of demarcation between the victim and the perpetrator is not always possible. As Nico Botha (1998:18) observes, it would be reductionist to say that the victims of apartheid were so totally paralysed that they could do very little to stop apartheid. Instead, he acknowledged the need for victims to confess that they did not do enough to stop apartheid. Human relationships that are extended over time are typically more complex than that.

The same applies to inter-group conflict. Consider the example of gangsters. It would be appropriate to suggest that gangsters are victims of economic and social forces far beyond their own control. Gangsterism on the Cape Flats may be regarded as a function of forced removals under the Group Areas act, economic deprivation, educational disadvantages, drugs trafficking and so on and so forth. At the same time gangsters also commit horrendous crimes (such as gang rape) where the vulnerable in society are further victimised. Add to that the violations of human rights that occur in the name of protection of the neighbourhood, self-defence, vengeance and an ensuing spiral of killing. In short, such gangsters are both victims and perpetrators. The same could probably be said of most criminals.[54] The parents of such gangsters may be affected by ongoing violence, they may feel

---

54 One may argue that the ministry of Jesus of Nazareth responded precisely to this problem. He addressed the needs of people who suffered under imperial oppression and rightly regarded themselves as victims. However, Jesus also recognised an underlying problem, namely the lack of solidarity and caring within Jewish society. This was aggravated by faction fighting associated with the different responses to imperial occupation amongst Sadducees, Pharisees, Zealots and Essenes. He started a liberation movement among the outcasts of his day, but nevertheless called them (the victims, those who are sinned against!) to repentance and conversion, since he recognised the dangers of a perpetuation of oppression, perhaps because the oppressed may envy the power of the oppressors.

See also Volf (1996: 114): "The truly revolutionary character of Jesus' proclamation lies precisely in the connection between the hope he gives to the oppressed and the radical change he requires of them. Though some sins have been imputed to them, other sins of theirs were real; though they suffered at the sinful hand of others, they also committed sins of their own. It is above all to them that he offered divine forgiveness." Volf adds: "[T]alk about the need for the victim's repentance has to do with the creation of the kind of social agents that are shaped by the values of God's kingdom and therefore capable of participating in the project of authentic social transformation" (1996:118).

responsible (and guilty) for the formation of their children's characters, and may even benefit from the "protection" offered by a gang. Clearly, tidy and categorical distinctions will not always do.[55] Moreover, from the point of view of therapy and pastoral counselling, the language of victimhood shows a pernicious tendency to undermine human agency and to disempower actual victims (see Volf 1996:103).

Reflection on the proportionality of guilt obviously becomes highly sensitive in the case of HIV infection. If one considers the stigmatisation of HIV-infected persons in society and in the church ("AIDS is God's punishment for promiscuity"), it would be appropriate to use the term "victim" in this regard. Consider also the stark statistics indicating that being faithful to one's husband is no guarantee against HIV infection in the South African context. However, to avoid using terms such as "guilt" in the context of HIV infection would be inappropriate, precisely because of such statistics. This example indicates how complex and dangerous the notion of the proportionality of guilt may be. Overtly, the husband is to be blamed, but one may easily find a situation where the wife would blame herself, for example, for not being "sexually available" in order to attend to her husband's "sexual needs". Such stereotypes may, of course, be entrenched through structures of patriarchy and religious notions of submission. Yet the least one can say is that the infidelity of the husband is a symptom of an already distorted relationship. If so, reflection on the proportionality rather than the rough equality of guilt is exactly what is required, however difficult that may be, precisely in order to preclude an equalising of such guilt.

On this basis one may observe that there is a tendency to speak too easily of purely innocent victims,[56] as if this infection may be treated medically

---

55 MM Thomas, the former moderator of the WCC's Central Committee, once observed that the lines dividing oppressors from the oppressed are always blurred: "When compared to the West, I am a victim; when compared to the poor of India, I am a victimizer. Beyond that, the question overlooks the reality of divine forgiveness, which enables the oppressed to trust and the oppressor to repent and which is always breaking in and transforming our world" (quoted in Kinnamon 2003:118).

56 Fraser Watts (2004:58) radicalises this insight by suggesting that we are implicated in every crime. There is no innocent party to a divorce, no accused

like any other viral infection and as if self-help therapy would suffice to heal broken relationships. Moreover, in an age of sexual license one does not need the word "promiscuity" to recognise the foolishness of reckless sexual affairs or visiting prostitutes. Clearly, some who have contracted the virus have to accept responsibility for that. They are both responsible for their own situation and victims of the pandemic.

In order to gain some clarity in reflection on the proportionality of guilt, a distinction between various forms of causation may be helpful. To establish a causal relationship with any degree of certainty is very difficult, especially in the social sciences. Aristotle's distinction between material, formal, efficient and final causes suggests that there are multiple levels of causation. Another distinction is between necessary, contributing and decisive factors. There are several factors that are necessary for me to make a cup of rooibos tea, including the availability of such tea leaves where I am, potable water, energy and cups, but one may add numerous others such as appropriate rainfall, soil conditions, farmers, distributers, the earth's gravity, the sun, etc. Electricity is a contributing but not a necessary factor, as I may also use a gas stove while camping to make this tea.

Amongst the almost endless necessary and contributing factors one needs to identify the decisive factor. This is where differences of opinion typically emerge. For example: the doctor may attribute the cause of a boy's death to drowning. His friend may blame himself for challenging the boy to swim to the wreck. The swimming coach at school may say that he should have trained the boys harder. His mother may blame herself for allowing the children to go to the beach on their own. The father may blame the incident on an emphasis on the wrong virtues in the education of boys, or perhaps for being an absent father. [57] In each case a decisive factor is identified but in very different ways.

---

who is not also an accuser, no offender who has not been offended. If so, it is difficult to offer forgiveness if we are always already involved in the failures of other people. Precisely since this cannot but blur the distinction between victim and perpetrator, it is necessary to speak about the proportionality of guilt.

57 This example is derived from Brümmer (2007:287-293), drawing on the work of John Lucas.

One may use this analysis to reflect on the causes of a broken relationship and the proportionality of guilt. What are the contributing factors that led to the breach? Which of these factors may be regarded as decisive? Who should accept responsibility for that? It is such responsibility that lies at the core of the need to speak about the proportionality of guilt. This is crucial in order to respond to the pastoral recognition that most people approach confession, as Villa-Vicencio (2002:11) observes, "with a mixture of repentance, self-defence, a measure of self-justification, reluctance and a desire to see the other person(s) show an equal amount of introspection and humility". He adds that this situation becomes even more complex where former perpetrators (or beneficiaries) see themselves as victims (for example, of affirmative action) in a changed political landscape. Moreover, victims may begin to cling onto their victimhood, since that may entitle them to attention and sympathy. In South Africa this has led to a disastrous (and consumerist) culture of entitlement (even including sexual entitlement), where those who regard themselves as "previously disadvantaged" may use that label as an excuse by "blaming everything on apartheid". The term "victim" may therefore need to be used with circumspection, since it disempowers the agency of the person by reducing him or her to that status.

As the examples above illustrate, reflection on the proportionality of guilt is necessary but also dangerous. It is best approached through pastoral counselling. The point of such counselling cannot be to calculate such proportionality. That would be possible only in cases where compensation can be quantified in financial terms. The aim of such counselling would rather be to identify and acknowledge the factors contributing to the breach in the relationship so that these factors can be dealt with by focusing on the perceived decisive factors. Once that is done, it is also necessary to address the emotions, perceptions and attitudes evoked in response to such contributing factors. Whenever there is a deficit that has to be addressed, only symbolic actions would suffice to address the situation – but only once the decisive factors have been identified and only once reparation has taken place, once what can be given back has been given back.

Discourse on confessing guilt in South Africa

In South Africa, divided by decades of apartheid, the role of storytelling is often emphasised as crucial for the recognition of guilt. Guilt cannot be discovered merely through self-examination. It is only through hearing the stories of others that you can discover what you have done and what you have been condoning. This is indeed crucial for the sake of a "healing of memories".

In the 1980s, when the social and political system of apartheid became more unstable and its flaws apparent, there emerged, at least in some Christian circles, a discourse on the notion of confessing guilt in South Africa. There were many questions: Who should confess guilt? Why? To what end? To whom? Where? When?

In an attempt to grapple with these questions several South African theologians investigated similarities to, and differences from, confessing guilt in Germany after World War II. Here the theology of Dietrich Bonhoeffer was especially inspirational. German documents such as the Stuttgart Confession of Guilt of the Synod of the Evangelical Church in October 1945 and the Darmstadt Declaration of 8 August 1947 were studied. What was striking in these German confessions, controversial as they were, is that those who confessed their guilt were people who fought against Nazism and suffered greatly in the process. They confessed their guilt, in the famous words of the Stuttgart declaration, "for not witnessing more courageously, for not praying more faithfully, for not believing more joyously and for not loving more ardently" (see De Gruchy 1989:34). They were not judging the nation, but expressed solidarity with the nation in their suffering and in their guilt. They accused themselves, not others.

The famous analysis by Karl Jaspers of four different types of guilt in *Die Schuldfrage* (1946) was often discussed in this South African discourse on confessing guilt (see especially De Gruchy 1993). Jaspers distinguished between criminal guilt, political guilt, moral guilt and metaphysical guilt. In terms of this analysis, the Truth and Reconciliation Commission addressed primarily criminal guilt (perpetrators of gross violations of human rights). The South African discourse on confessing guilt in the 1980s grappled especially with the political and moral forms of guilt. "Confessing guilt" was a term used especially in three contexts, namely the Dutch Reformed Church,[58] the National Initiative for Reconciliation[59] and, more controversially, also within the South African Council of Churches (SACC). The debate within the SACC is particularly interesting.

The SACC hosted a conference on confessing guilt in 1988 on the basis of the conviction that the time had already arrived to lay the foundations for a post-apartheid South Africa. This discourse on confessing guilt was very controversial at the time. There was a sense that an emphasis on confessing guilt may weaken, endanger or even jeopardise the struggle for freedom and democracy. What the oppressed needed most was not to seek reconciliation with repentant oppressors, but liberation from oppression.

This has to be understood against the background of the Kairos Document (1985), which denounced talk about reconciliation as "church theology". Moreover, there was a genuine fear that white Christians might hijack a public confession of guilt to obtain a cheap form of grace without justice. This would have put the oppressed – who would be called upon to forgive those who have confessed their guilt – in an unbearable position. Yet there was also the recognition that the confession of guilt, repentance and conversion is fundamental to the nature of Christian life and indeed crucial to overcome the hatred and bitterness caused by decades of apartheid. The question was therefore what a confession of guilt could mean. Here a number of layers could be identified.

Firstly, the National Conference of the SACC adopted a resolution in 1985 which reads: "The Conference believes that there is a need for confession of guilt by white Christians for the unjust structures they have inflicted upon the black people of this land and requests the

---

58 There is an extensive literature on confessing guilt within this context. See especially Bosch, König and Nicol (1982). See also the famous confession of guilt by Prof. Willie Jonker in Alberts and Chikane (1991:92).

59 See especially Nürnberger and Tooke (1988).

Division of Mission and Evangelism to devise ways and means of assisting individuals and congregations to come to this point" (Finca *et al.* 1989:13). The emphasis here is on those Christians who actively supported apartheid, identified in overtly racial terms. The primary focus was the ways in which the policies of apartheid were actively and insistently propagated by the Dutch Reformed Church in the 1930s and the 1940s. However, this category also included those who ignored the evils associated with apartheid, who spiritualised the gospel and maintained a separation between church and society. Moreover, those who denounced apartheid, but who were rather slow in doing so, were also called to confess, since this allowed the status quo to prevail for too long.

Secondly, there was also a sense in which mainline churches supported apartheid, either actively, or through being themselves divided along racial lines, or through complicity and silence, or through not being courageous enough in resisting the system. The divisions since 1857 and 1881 between the various branches of the Dutch Reformed Church on the basis of race and ethnicity not only served as a kind of prototype for the apartheid policies that followed later, but were also copied by several other denominations. The 1987 National Conference of the SACC adopted a second resolution in this regard, now calling for a conference on the question "whether Christian people can unite in a Confession of Guilt for the past" (Finca *et al.* 1989:13). This was evidently awkward for many church leaders in the SACC, who had dedicated themselves to the struggle against apartheid, but who belonged to churches which failed to do that. As church leaders they could not quite distance themselves from this form of guilt. There was indeed a need for repentance for the disunity of churches in South Africa. While Christians confessed to be of one body, they continued to move in separate worlds. This indicated a tension between one's political identity and one's ecclesial identity. It was much easier to identify with like-minded political activists than with unrepentant fellow Christians. For some the church was indeed their primary reference group, while others saw the SACC pragmatically as a helpful ally in the struggle against apartheid.

Thirdly, there were controversial intimations regarding the guilt of the oppressed themselves. Of course, such a confession of guilt by the victim may have been easily abused by the oppressor. The danger was that the guilt of the victims could be seen as somehow on a par with the sins of the oppressors. Some nevertheless suggested that black Christians have to repent of their bitterness for what whites have done. Bongani Finca (1989:23) acknowledged at the time that there was a growing desire for revenge by a generation of blacks who had been so hurt and dehumanised that they have become possessed by a desire for revenge. The victim's guilt might have included various aspects: a failure of courage to fight against the system, responding to it with timidity and fear, looking for ways of escaping suffering through making compromises, acquiescing in oppression and accepting its dehumanising impact, failing to be instruments of peace amidst growing intolerance, hating the oppressor and wishing for the downfall of the oppressor (not only the downfall of the system), and not giving the oppressor the opportunity to change. During this time Desmond Tutu, for example, never stopped emphasising that there would be no liberation for the oppressed without the liberation of the oppressor.

Fourthly, the ferocious black-on-black violence raging in the South African townships at the time should also be taken into account. Such violence was symbolised by the infamous necklace method of executing informers. This should be understood against the background of resistance against various forms of collaborating with an evil system and therefore against any compromises within the ranks of the struggle activists against apartheid. Such animosity, suspicion and forms of violence naturally generated immense trauma and a sense of guilt.

Finally, there were also those who called for a vicarious confession of guilt. This has to be understood as a response to the human inclination towards self-affirmation and self-reliance, and therefore not to accept responsibility and not to confess guilt. It is common for those who are truly guilty to blame it on others, on orders from above, on adverse circumstances. Since many were unwilling to confess their own guilt for maintaining apartheid rule, it was suggested by some Christians that the church has a tremendous responsibility to confess not only its own guilt, but also the guilt of others, "to repent of it as if all the guilt is entirely the guilt of the church" (see Botha 1989:19). This kind of confession would indeed imply that the church would take all the guilt upon itself vicariously. When the church becomes willing to confess, on behalf of the world, the possibility of forgiveness arises.

This discourse on confessing guilt in South Africa culminated at the national conference of church leaders held in Rustenberg in November 1990. In the Rustenberg declaration there is a lengthy section on confession (of guilt). Here the church leaders confess that "we have in different ways practised, supported, permitted or refused to resist apartheid" (section 2.5).[60] The document then continues to spell out these different ways, covering the full range mentioned above. In terms of the notion of being beneficiaries of apartheid, these different ways are reflected in the following formulation: "we have been unwilling to suffer, loving our comfort more than God's justice and clinging to our privilege rather than binding ourselves to the poor and oppressed of our land."[61]

Contemplating forgiveness

Forgiveness plays a crucial role in the process of coming to terms with experiences of the violation of human dignity. In general, one may observe that something like forgiveness is necessary for a person to come to terms with the past in order to be liberated from feelings of vengeance and to be able to continue with her or his life with a view to the future. This requires "serendipity, imagination, risk and the exploration of what it means 'to start again'" (Villa-Vicencio 2002:4). In her book *The Human Condition* Hannah Arendt states the following:

---

60 See Alberts and Chikane (1991:277). See also the report by the Research Institute on Christianity in South Africa, commissioned by the Truth and Reconciliation Commission to advise the commission on its hearings dealing with submissions by faith communities. The report offers a thorough analysis of the various stances adopted by faith communities to apartheid. See "Faith Communities and apartheid: The RICSA report" in Cochrane, De Gruchy and Martin (1999:15-80).

61 See section 2.6 of the Rustenburg declaration in Alberts and Chikane (1991:278).

It needs forgiving, dismissing, in order to make possible for life to go on by constantly releasing men from what they have done unknowingly. Only through this constant mutual release from what they do can men remain free agents. Forgiving in other words is the only reaction, which does not merely re-act but acts anew and unexpectedly, unconditioned by the act which provoked it and therefore freeing from its consequences both the one who forgives and the one who is forgiven (1958:240).

In the same vein Desmond Tutu comments in *No future without forgiveness* (1999:220):

In the act of forgiveness we are declaring our faith in the future of a relationship and in the capacity of the wrongdoer to make a new beginning on a course that will be different from the one that caused us the wrong. We are saying here is a chance to make a new beginning. It is an act of faith that the wrongdoer can change.

The decision by a victim to verbally offer forgiveness to the perpetrator will obviously be influenced by the violation of the victim's dignity by the perpetrator and the subsequent events which transpired between the victim and the perpetrator. The following factors may play a role in this regard.

- The victim may come to the realisation that feelings of anger, resentment and vengeance will inhibit his or her ability to come to terms with the violation of human rights and to continue with life. In order to address such anger, resentment and vengeance, the victim may offer forgiveness to the perpetrator in order to put the episode behind her or him, i.e. in order to "forgive and forget", to find "closure"[62] for the trauma experienced.

62 Closure may be understood as "a psychological concept that is frequently mentioned as a desired end-state following any variety of psychological traumas and refers to a state of psychological resolution that is achieved when people feel they can effectively move beyond the trauma and attend to other problems and concerns" (quoted in Weinstein (2011:4). This emphasis on closure is questioned by Weinstein (2011) as a euphemism that does not take the lingering of corporate memories into account. Grunebaum-Ralph and Stier (1999:149) add that a reconciliation metanarrative should not be imposed upon memories of trauma, since it may take years for such memories to be articulated (in the light of examples from the Holocaust) and individual processes of coming to terms with the past necessarily remain fragmented. Even if such closure may be desirable, for healing to take place it should not be induced too quickly by mediators or therapists. The temporal axis of reconciliation is again crucial here. The healing

This is only possible if the victim who was left powerless as a result of an overwhelming force can find a response other than fear (and escape) or resistance (and retaliation).[63] The focus is therefore on the psychological healing of the victim[64] in order not to be held hostage by the pain of the past.[65]

- In addition, the victim may realise that resentment may provoke undesirable consequences in terms of the contemplation of acts of revenge. Such a contemplation of revenge is an understandable response to the suffering of loss and violation. Acts of revenge may lead to a destructive spiral of violence, which may have very serious consequences for the victim, which the victim may well recognise – and fear. However, even the contemplation of acts of revenge may hold the victim hostage to the past. To offer forgiveness to the perpetrator may therefore serve as an indication that the victim has consciously decided not to contemplate the possibility of revenge any longer. The focus here is therefore on the psychological and also the social circumstances of the victim. This decision may also be motivated by the psychological need for the "healing of memories".

- The victim may be satisfied that the perpetrator has been punished appropriately for the violation of human rights, even though the harm

---

of memories may take decades. Grunebaum-Ralph and Stier (1999:151-152) refer to the example of the Israelites who, after generations of slavery, took the bones of their ancestor Joseph to be buried in the promised land. They argue that the remembrance of collective trauma cannot be shifted easily into the mode of reconciliation: "The remains of the past must be borne into the present before they can be laid to rest in the service of a still deferred future."

63   See the discussion on trauma ("the affliction of the powerless") in Daye (2004:126-133).

64   In his popular book *Forgive and forget* Lewis Smedes suggests that one must forgive primarily for one's own sake, for the sake of one's own spiritual health and one's own future. The motivation for forgiveness is the happiness and health of those who do the forgiving. For a discussion, see Smit (1995:8f), who maintains, in contrast, that according to the Christian paradigm we do not forgive because we want to heal ourselves, but because we have been forgiven.

65   On a somewhat lighter note, I recall a conversation between my grandmother and a few of her friends. One of them told the others: "Stop complaining; it is now my turn to complain." There may be a reluctance to reach closure if recalling some past or present pain (e.g. from an operation) constitutes one's best claim to the attention and sympathy of others. It may eventually shape one's identity. Since, for example, I am the one who lost a child 70 years ago, I am entitled to your continued sympathy. If I relinquish this claim to attention I will lose more than the pain it causes me. Any trauma should be taken seriously (e.g. toddler hurting a finger), but healing also requires a sense of proportionality since one may indeed begin to treasure one's pain.

that was done to the victim(s) can never be undone. The victim is therefore satisfied that legal justice (but not necessarily restorative justice) has been served. In such a case, the willingness to offer forgiveness serves as an indication that the imbalances caused by the violation of human rights have been stabilised more or less as far as the victim is concerned. The focus here is on the status of the legal relationship between two citizens of a country who are not necessarily closely related to one another. It should be noted that this aspect would be problematic in cases where amnesty has been granted to the perpetrators within the context of the TRC processes.

- The victim may offer forgiveness to the perpetrator on the basis of a growing understanding for the circumstances within which the violation of human rights occurred. In the context of the struggle against apartheid in South Africa, the victim may realise that violations of human rights may have been politically motivated and that there would necessarily be victims of such long-term political conflict. This does not imply that particular gross violations of human rights may be condoned, but that the larger interests of establishing democracy, national reconciliation and nation building outweigh the harm suffered by the individual victim. The focus here would be on the place of the victim within the larger social and political context of civil society.

- The victim may offer forgiveness to the perpetrator on the basis of a growing understanding of the perpetrator and the more immediate circumstances under which the violation of human rights occurred. In this case the victim may recognise in the perpetrator a fallible human being who is at least partially the product of circumstances beyond his or her own control. The perpetrator is therefore no longer regarded as an alien other but as a fellow human being. In addition, the victim may recognise the ways in which the violation of human rights may have had a detrimental impact on the perpetrator's life too. To offer forgiveness to the perpetrator may therefore be based on a peculiar sense of empathy or mercy felt by the victim for the perpetrator and the willingness to offer a second chance to the perpetrator. The focus here is on the psychological and social circumstances of the perpetrator. This requires a magnanimous attitude from the victim to be willing to place herself or himself in the shoes of the perpetrator.

- The willingness to offer forgiveness may be based on the recognition by the victim of authentic signs of repentance, a confession of guilt, remorse and a willingness to offer some appropriate form of restoration in the body language, words and actions of the perpetrator.[66] To offer forgiveness within such circumstances would indicate a recognition by the victim of

---

66 Russell Daye (2004:15) identifies five possibilities for forgiving someone who has willingly harmed me: 1) he repented and had a change of heart; 2) his motives

the need to restore a broken relationship with the perpetrator (if one did not exist in the past, it does so now). This would imply that appropriate acts of reparation (as far as this would be possible) might well be expected by the victim from the perpetrator. This would be especially appropriate in a context where the victim and the perpetrator are relatively closely related to one another (e.g. family members, neighbours, colleagues, or affiliation to non-governmental, community or faith-based organisations.)

It should be clear that what is understood by "offering forgiveness" will not be the same in each of these cases. While theological reflection on forgiveness typically focuses on a richer notion of forgiveness that will lead to reconciliation and the flourishing of relationships, this is not necessarily the same in secular discourse on forgiveness.

One crucial question that arises here is whether forgiveness may indeed be regarded as "unconditional".[67] In the theological discourse on forgiveness it is usually said that forgiveness can only be offered if it is unconditional. To be liberating, forgiveness has to be offered freely or not at all. This implies that remorse, contrition or reparation cannot be stipulated as conditions for forgiveness (see Tutu 1999:220). On the contrary, it may well be the experience of God's forgiveness or the magnanimity of the victim's forgiveness that prompts the perpetrator's remorse.

The complexity of the process of contemplating forgiveness as sketched above suggests that forgiveness has to be situated within a longer narrative commencing with a prior relationship (even if between strangers) and ending with the nature of an anticipated future relationship. It should be clear that reconciliation in the form of fellowship is not possible without offering and receiving forgiveness. However, the locus of forgiveness in the narrative can be situated differently and cannot be prescribed. It may be shaped by unresolved past memories and anticipated reciprocity.

---

were actually good; 3) he has suffered enough; 4) he has undergone humiliation; 5) a recollection of past friendship, "for old times' sake".

67 The *Kairos Document* (1985) maintained that "The Biblical teaching on reconciliation and forgiveness makes it quite clear that nobody can be forgiven and reconciled with God unless he or she repents of their sins. Nor are we expected to forgive the unrepentant sinner." However, as Brümmer (2005:43) also observes, repentance is indeed a condition for reconciliation but not necessarily for forgiveness.

In all cases offering forgiveness is open-ended and entails a temporal axis. To offer forgiveness is an act of courage and risk-taking, since the response from the other cannot be guaranteed. At the very least offering forgiveness anticipates an appropriate response. That response may or may not lead to the flourishing of a prior relationship.

If that is the case, forgiveness may in some cases be offered only subsequent to acts of reparation, compensation and also punishment (forgiveness for the deficit does not exclude the legitimacy of punishment). What can be given back should be given back before forgiveness (for the remaining deficit) can be offered.[68] In other cases forgiveness can only be offered following the perpetrator's remorse and in anticipation of a reciprocal response (the cases studies recorded in the proceedings of the South African TRC provide ample examples). In yet other cases (such as the forgiveness offered by a parent) forgiveness may cover any need for reparation, compensation and restitution (thus going far beyond the deficit) and may be offered unconditionally in the hope of an appropriate response. Stephen Cherry (2004:174) rightly observes that this depends very much on the prior relationship. In cases where an intimate relationship existed beforehand, forgiveness that is offered early signals the desire to perpetuate the relationship. In cases where no such close relationship existed, delaying forgiveness may be appropriate: to bring closure prematurely may remove the need for a longer-term relationship in which a more profound reconciliation based on justice and reciprocity may emerge. In fact, an apology met by an appropriate response would bring closure to mutual obligations and thus to the relationship itself.

---

68 Desmond Tutu recalls the case of Brian Mitchell in the proceedings of the TRC. The victims in this case, namely a rural community from the Trust Feed Farm, were willing to forgive the perpetrators provided that Mitchell became actively involved in reconstructing the community he had helped to destroy (Tutu 1999:137). Is forgiveness here understood as conditional? Or is the anticipated response on the basis of a willingness to forgive merely stipulated? Or is the moral suspense created by the reluctance to forgive indeed very healthy (Watts & Gulliford 2004:171)? Tutu (1999:138) comments that such reparation perhaps should have been required before amnesty was granted in all other cases in the proceedings of the TRC! That would follow confessional practices with respect to appropriate forms of penance!

A differentiated understanding of forgiveness is necessary in order to address two problems that plague prospects for reconciliation.

- Firstly, victims often find it difficult to cope with lasting memories of atrocities. Even where forgiveness is offered, the "affliction of memory" (Volf 1996:131) does not disappear and constantly remind survivors not only of the horror but also of injustices and the costs of reconciliation that have to be borne by the victim. Even where forgiveness is offered unconditionally, the victim may have to contemplate whether the offer was indeed genuine, given such feelings of resentment. Recalling past atrocities would place that continuously in doubt.

- Secondly, forgiveness as an act of courage is offered precisely in anticipation of a reciprocal response that would level the playing fields. What if such a response is not forthcoming? The courage of the victim to offer forgiveness is not recognised, the burden carried by the victim is not appreciated or underestimated, and the rapprochement (Afrikaans: toenadering) is rejected. Insult is added to injury. This will provoke the anger of the victim, who may well respond with feelings of hurt and vengeance not commensurate with the magnanimity that characterised the offer of forgiveness in the immediate past. This kind of response is also typical of distorted sexual relationships. If one's approach with sexual innuendos (e.g. to make up after some conflict) is rejected by one's partner, this may provoke an unreasonable anger that belies the intended intimacy, but is nevertheless indicative of how such an approach renders one vulnerable. Of course, a premature approach also indicates a lack of sensitivity to one's partner's intimate space and signals a lack of reciprocity in the relationship.

In both cases the forgiveness that was offered is thwarted. On this basis it is again crucial to recognise the temporal axis of offering forgiveness in the process of reconciliation. Forgiveness should be offered at the right moment, not too soon and not too late, so that there is little delay between the experience of forgiveness and a reciprocal response. When there is a longer delay, this would require not only magnanimity but also patience and long-suffering. Such virtues set the bar for reconciliation very high indeed.

Reconciliation and anticipated restitution

In South African theological discourse on reconciliation the dangers of "cheap reconciliation" have been widely recognised. This is epitomised by the critique of the *Kairos Document* regarding the emphasis on reconciliation in what it denounced as "church theology". In a theological statement on reconciliation issued by the National Initiative for Reconciliation (see Nürnberger & Tooke 1988:87) the danger of such cheap reconciliation in "church theology" is recognised with heightened sensitivity:

> However, reconciliation which serves to conceal or play down injustices, which condones the abuse of power at the expense of others, which appeases the wronged party, which expects of the victims of structural imbalances to accept their fate, which serves to avoid the suffering necessary for the restoration or development of just relationships, or which assigns to one party more of the benefits and to another more of the sacrifices is a fraud and stands condemned in the eyes of God and human morality. It will make no contribution to the resolution of conflict and undermines the credibility and effectiveness of the church's message of reconciliation in society.

In response to this view, the link between reconciliation and justice is also widely recognised. This is epitomised by the third and fourth articles of the Confession of Belhar, where both justice and reconciliation are emphasised. Or it is evident in the subtitle of John de Gruchy's study (2002), reconciliation means restoring justice, i.e. restorative justice.[69] Yet perceptions remain equally widespread that "reconciliation" may all too easily become a slogan emphasised by those who allow inequalities to be perpetuated. As a result, it is still widely questioned whether reconciliation can indeed serve as one of the guiding visions for South Africa beyond apartheid. This scepticism is best expressed in the tension between the work of the Truth and Reconciliation Commission and the reality that South Africa remains economically one of the most unequal societies in the world. It thus seems that the term "reconciliation" can only be maintained if "cheap reconciliation" can be contrasted with "radical reconciliation" (Boesak & DeYoung 2012).

---

69 Elsewhere De Gruchy (1988:169) suggests that the struggle for justice is aimed at reconciliation, while justice forms the basis for the very possibility of reconciliation.

One may observe that this tension between "cheap" and "radical" reconciliation is related to a tension embedded in the very nature of reconciliation. On the one hand, reconciliation is only possible between equals (Boesak & DeYoung 2012:20). In relationships previously characterised by oppression, reconciliation can therefore only occur on the basis of the liberation of both the oppressed and the oppressor. Reconciliation without liberation is indeed impossible (Boesak & DeYoung 2012:22). This applies to different kinds of relationships, i.e. between individuals, groups, institutions, churches, parties and countries.

The emphasis on equity has several connotations. First, it requires a recognition of a similar legal status and mutual respect for that status. It requires a mutual recognition of one another's inalienable human dignity. This does not imply equity in all respects as relationships characterised by a form of inequality can still be based on mutual respect and dignity (e.g. between parents and children, teachers and students, employers and employees). Second, it obviously entails a mutual concern for one another's interests. Each party has to be given what is due to them. That typically implies the need for acts of reparation and compensation. Third, it implies that suffering be shared, that the suffering of the one is carried by the other as far as this is possible and appropriate. In some cases this requires appropriate forms of punishment (retributive justice). It may also be addressed through voluntary acts of restitution by the perpetrator or by the beneficiaries of previous forms of inequality. Fourth, it implies the need for shared responsibilities, for helping one another. This does not necessarily imply equal responsibility, but the responsibility to contribute to the common wellbeing according to one's ability and position (contributive justice). Directors of companies thus have more responsibilities compared to others in management or workers. Finally, it implies the need for reciprocal giving and a willingness to receive gifts from the other, which places one in the other's debt.

The last aspect may well offer a test case for mutual respect. The rich often find it hard to receive something from the poor, or to recognise that the poor have something to give them besides their (cheap) labour. The same applies to many other relationships characterised by inequality. Paternalism, for example, has to be recognised for what it is and resisted. In a telling observation Steve Biko noted that there were some whites who participated in the struggle and had "black souls wrapped in white skins". However, it felt like they "always knew what was good for blacks and told them so" (quoted in Boesak & DeYoung 2012:20). Humility is therefore a prerequisite for equity.

On the other hand, reconciliation is impossible without forgiveness. This is related to the role of the deficit as discussed above. What can be given back should be given back through acts of reparation. However, there is always a deficit that cannot be given back. This can still be addressed through acts of restitution (see below), but even then a deficit will remain, if only because experiences of harm that was done can never be undone; only the impact of that harm can be addressed. Reconciliation is only possible if that deficit is forgiven by the victim. That is why reconciliation is costly. It implies suffering: the victim has to be willing to carry that additional and disproportionate burden. Moreover, the risk of offering forgiveness makes the victim vulnerable yet again, in this instance to the anticipated response of the perpetrator (see below). Forgiveness is offered by the victim for the sake of restoring a relationship that has become distorted through injustices. Complete equality is therefore not possible if reconciliation is to take place. In any flourishing relationship any new act of giving and receiving will disturb the equilibrium and puts the one in the debt of the other. In any healthy relationship a rough equilibrium would normally suffice.[70] Full justice cannot ever be done and in healthy relationships need not be done.

---

70 Nürnberger (1988:116-117) raises the question of whether this also applies in structural terms in liberal societies. Given liberal notions of freedoms, competition is welcomed as long as the opportunity of others to compete is not precluded. Where this does happen, hierarchies of power emerge through which injustices become embedded in society. Whatever reconciliation may mean in structural terms, those who have managed to gain positions of status and power (e.g. monopolies, political control) have to relinquish such positions of power in order to allow others a chance to compete. If so, the price for reconciliation has to be paid by the powerful, which is seldom done voluntarily. Of course, those who have been victims of structural injustices have to pay the price of such

The problem is, of course, that this recognition that reconciliation requires forgiveness (and an additional burden on the victim) can easily be abused by the former perpetrator to maintain inequalities and past privileges. If so, there can be no reconciliation based on mutual respect, since the willingness of the victim to carry the burden for the sake of the relationship is not appreciated by the perpetrator (or any beneficiaries). This leads to a continuation of strained relationships. As Desmond Tutu (1999:221) observes, "the huge gap between the haves and have-nots ... poses the greatest threat to reconciliation and stability in our country." The perpetrator can even demand forgiveness or expect further sacrifices to be made by the other. The victim may sometimes be willing to carry such an additional burden but this will heighten the tension and the anxiety in awaiting a reciprocal response. This may again be abused. A continuation of unequal relationships based on a willingness to make sacrifices is the subject of feminist and postcolonial critiques. Understandably, the victim may in such cases begin to see forgiveness as conditional. Accordingly, I will only forgive you if your anticipated response will prove to be appropriate. However, this would confuse forgiveness and reconciliation. Forgiveness can only take place unconditionally. Reconciliation is not based on forgiveness alone, but on the building of relationships based on mutual respect and reciprocity. Reconciliation, by contrast, has several associated conditions, including reparation, forgiveness and restitution.

The underlying problem here is one of risk-taking and the anticipation by the victim of an appropriate response from the perpetrator. Offering forgiveness undeniably implies the victim taking a risk, since this will perpetuate the inequality that characterised a distorted relationship. The victim has to bear a disproportionate share of the burdens and suffering. However, since forgiveness is offered precisely for the sake of the relationship, this is always accompanied by anticipation of what an appropriate reciprocal response might entail. There is a necessary delay between taking such a risk and awaiting a response. This creates tension and anxiety. If such an appropriate and hopefully surprising

---

domination, but prospects for "reconciliation" would bring no further costs, only enhanced opportunities.

response were not forthcoming, this would lead to resentment as the victim then recognises that her or his willingness to carry the additional burden is not appreciated by the perpetrator. The victim would then tend to demand acts of compensation or restitution, if only for the sake of maintaining self-respect. Of course, there may be a fine line between the anticipation of an appropriate reciprocal response and the demand for such a response. Often such an anticipated response is disappointing for the victim. The end result is that reconciliation is frustrated and thwarted, making further attempts at reconciliation difficult, since the sincerity of confessing guilt or of offering forgiveness anew is then necessarily questioned. Reconciliation is elusive precisely because it is only possible when forgiveness is offered unconditionally, when the tension is maintained through anticipation, when an appropriate reciprocal response is forthcoming, and when that leads to a long process of mutual sharing, giving and receiving.

It is in this context that the crucial role of restitution has to be recognised. As suggested above, it is best to make a distinction between reparation and restitution. Reparation refers to the need to give back what can be given back, or to offer compensation for what cannot be given back. This is a minimum requirement for justice and also for reconciliation. Where that is not forthcoming, reconciliation is not possible. It is also not possible to offer forgiveness in such a context, if forgiveness is understood as the willingness to take a risk to restore a relationship based on mutual respect. Offering forgiveness without reparation would merely perpetuate inequalities. Of course, it may still be possible to offer forgiveness even without any form of reparation (and without signs of remorse or a confession of guilt). Such magnanimity would heighten the tension, temporarily increase the inequality in the relationship and add moral weight to the anticipated response. In that case reparation would still have to follow forgiveness in order to restore a relationship characterised by reciprocity and equity. Reconciliation is only possible on that basis.

If reparation can be used in this way,[71] restitution then refers to ways of addressing the lasting deficit once the need for reparation and compensation has been addressed. Such restitution includes forms of restoration that address less tangible aspects such as human dignity, personal status, common memories, opportunities and participation. The problem of course is that it is often not possible to distinguish so carefully between reparation, compensation and restitution, precisely given the nature of the deficit. Relationships that have become distorted over a longer period of time are often more complicated than that. It is then no longer clear what can indeed be given back and to whom it should be given back. In the special case of amnesty, the victim loses the right to sue for civil damages in compensation from the perpetrator. It thus legally induces the burden upon the victim (see Tutu 1999:52) so that such compensation is added to the deficit. Moreover, whereas amnesty comes into effect immediately, there is always a time-delay between conferring amnesty on the perpetrator and the victim receiving compensation.

In the *Restitution Toolkit* developed by the Restitution Foundation the following scenario is sketched to illustrate the problem of determining what reparation entails:

> Imagine this scenario: a man's bicycle is stolen. This now means he has no transport and cannot get to work; thus he loses his job. Without a job, he cannot educate his children or support his family. Perhaps he used that bicycle to run errands for the homebound elderly woman next door; now she is affected by the loss as well. Jobless and frustrated, he becomes a drain on his community rather than a resource. What would restitution look like in this situation? Certainly it is not just returning the bicycle. He is not the only person who has been affected by the crime; his family, his neighbours and his community have also suffered. Now imagine that theft not only of resources such as land, education and money has occurred on a broad scale, but also of intangibles: dignity, a sense of safety, self-

---

71 This term is used in different ways in the literature. Daye (2004:140-141) suggests instead that "reparation" may be used as a generic term that could then include restitution (to re-establish the former situation as far as possible), compensation, rehabilitation (including various forms of care) and satisfaction (guarantees introduced to prevent the repetition of human rights violations).

worth, an understanding of one's rights, a sense of belonging in one's own country (Snyman 2012:8-9).[72]

The impact of past injustices, especially in the form of structural violence, is made even more complex by the way that suppressed responses to trauma are deferred only to re-emerge in other contexts. This is well understood in folk psychology: if one is angry with one's boss or if one has experienced injustices at work about which little can be done, the anger can be expressed elsewhere in disconnected areas where one can still exercise control, e.g. by kicking the dog at home or in the form of domestic violence. There is surely a correlation between the trauma of apartheid – especially the way adult men were stripped of their manliness and dignity (even by white children) – and the current levels of violence against women. This obviously cannot be used as a rationale to condone such violence against women and children. To find appropriate forms of restitution in such a context, where new violations of human rights have to be addressed as well, becomes highly complex (Daye 2004:130).

What, then, does restitution entail? The *Restitution Toolkit* suggests this: "Restitution involves seeking to set right the generational ills of inequality by engaging those who have benefited from the system, directly or indirectly, in transferring wealth and social capital and reinvesting in communities that still suffer from the past's grim legacy" (Snyman 2012:49). It adds that restitution is not *charity*. Charity assumes a relationship in which there is a clear benefactor and a clear beneficiary, roles that still leave power on one side and that can be unintentionally dehumanising.[73]

---

72 See the reading of the story of Zacchaeus in Boesak and DeYoung (2012:57-74). Zacchaeus paid back to the victims four times what he has stolen from them (Luke 19:8). One may suggest that this entails reparation, compensation (for lost opportunities) and also restitution for the sake of reconciliation with his fellow citizens. Boesak and DeYoung (2012:70) adds that reconciliation is not possible without a sense of public shame. However, "the sense of shame turns into an internal pit of paralyzing self-abuse and self-pity if it is not turned into redemptive deeds of justice and restitution."

73 The *Restitution Toolkit* comments: "Charity can also be an assault on the dignity of the recipient. She has not been asked her needs, but rather had them diagnosed for her. She has not been asked why she is in the situation she is, why

Reconciliation requires some form of *restoration* (in the sense of restorative justice – see Tutu 1999:51), although that is rather deceptive, since it seems to suggest that there was some previous time in which parties lived in harmony and had relations with each other characterised by mutual respect. Yet that is typically not the case, especially if much time has passed since the injustices were committed and if the former relationship was not desirable in the first place (e.g. patriarchy, colonialism, imperialism).

Here again understanding the influence on reconciliation of the passage of time is vital. Transitoriness not only plays a role in understanding the deficit (time that was "lost" or filled with memories of injustices), but also in contemplating the possibilities of restoring relationships that have been affected in the interim by death, old age, fragility, disability and historical change, especially in societies characterised by "rapid social change". The question is therefore what the "re-" might entail in words such as "restoration" (to have something available, in

---

her community is suffering, and what she thinks the solution is. She is simply reminded again that she lacks, while others have plenty" (Snyman 2012:18-19).

See also the stringent critique by Allan Boesak of the condescending and "unbearably racist" overtones evident in the following letter by a young woman on what white people are doing for blacks in this country that was published in an Afrikaans daily newspaper: "We GIVE! We take care (of them), we provide, we share, we cook soup and bake bread for them, empty our closets, we 'tip' the shop assistant who helps us and the parking assistant and at the car wash. We pay for the funerals of their extended families to the third generation. We pay their school fees ... We train our domestic servants, we knit jerseys, caps and gloves; we buy blankets, give our food away along the roads. We teach them to be neat, to pick up their trash, to cook, make clothes, to plant, to farm, to milk cows. We GIVE! We buy birthday cakes, medicine, pay their taxi fare, give our precious food to their hungry children. We stop the car and give them candy. We GIVE! We create jobs, we pity them, we pray, we pick up their babies from trash cans and bring them up, we organise parties at crèches in squatter camps ... we give (our) hearts, livers, kidneys, lungs and tongues. We GIVE! We are not racist, nor vengeful, (despite everything) we remain in our country, we clean up after them, ferry them around. We comfort them, explain, remain calm, patiently waiting in long lines and smile ... We GIVE! Did I say it already? We GIVE!" Boesak rightly comments that this understanding of generosity "treats black people as helpless, wretched children, perpetual beggars, ingrates who scarcely deserve the charity white people dole out on a daily basis". It also fails to address the historical link between the beneficiaries and the victims of apartheid (in Boesak and DeYoung 2012:145-146).

store again), "reconciliation" (to be together again), "renewal" (to make something new again), "reconstruction" (to construct something again within existing parameters) or restitution (to re-establish the shape of something[74]). What is restored is not the relationship itself but something about that relationship.

What that "something" might entail is perhaps more a question of imagining new possibilities for the future than of returning to a previous dispensation. This applies obviously in cases where no significant previous relationship actually existed, for example, in the case of road accidents, the rape of strangers or the influx of foreigners. In South Africa this is a pertinent issue because of the role of land redistribution in national reconciliation. It is clear that some form of restoration is required, but it is far from clear what timeframe for restoration would be applicable (from 1948, 1913, 1910, 1834, 1652, 1492 or 100 000 years ago?). Note that these dates (except for the last) are linked to forms of domination as a result of the influx of foreigners who came to stay and became interwoven with the ongoing migrations of people who were here at that time. It is scarcely possible to undo such history or to call on such foreigners to "go home". Of course, this recognition may easily become an excuse for the beneficiaries of the injustices of history to protect current privileges through inaction on the basis of the complexities of restitution.

It may therefore be more appropriate to speak of transitional or transformational justice that recognises the need for establishing and building new relationships (Snyman 2012:7).[75] Transitional justice at the very least seeks to prevent the recurrence of human rights violations, attends to distributive justice and encourages the promotion of

---

74 The word "restitution" is derived the Latin *statuere*, meaning "to establish". One of the connotations listed by *The Concise Oxford Dictionary* is the "resumption of original shape or position because of elasticity".

75 According to Daye (2004:113-122), the objectives of transitional justice include the following: 1) the restoration and celebration of the dignity of victims; 2) the implementation of measures to ensure accountability; 3) the entrenchment, upholding and protection of human rights; 4) the implementation of measures to advance distributive justice; 5) the prevention of revenge taking and other forms of violence; and 6) the pursuit of reconciliation.

educational and job opportunities (Daye 2004:112). This has to be done in innovative and imaginative ways in contexts where relationships have become strained over long periods of time. Moreover, restitution is not only needed with respect to a particular incident where, or period when, harm was done in the past and is now being addressed (backward-looking restitution). It is also needed to address processes through which injustices will prevail and be reinforced without specific interventions (forward-looking restitution). Indeed, beyond the contested terrain may well be common grounds where a meeting of minds is possible. Strategies for such interventions may include a differentiated tax basis, budget allocations, "black empowerment" and affirmative action. They may cover different timeframes, in some cases extending over a generation or more – which may be required in cases where injustices became embedded in structural violence that extended over centuries. It is preferable that such timeframes and their termination dates be clarified from the outset. Each of the following forms of backward-looking restitution related to structural injustices perpetrated in the period between 1652 and 1994 would have to be addressed for the sake of "national reconciliation", but then in different ways and according to different timeframes, taking into account in what ways and to what extent these aspects have been shaped by past injustices:

- The need for a more equitable distribution of land amongst current citizens;

- The need for some form of housing provided to all citizens in order to restore the possibility of family life;

- The availability of sufficient fresh water and basic sanitation to all citizens;

- The availability of basic food products at affordable prices;

- The availability of primary health care to all citizens;

- The availability of adequate basic education opportunities for all citizens;

- The need to allow all willing adult citizens to contribute to the country's wellbeing through their labour (to address the possibility of contributive justice);

- The need to adjust salary scales (if need be through taxes) so that the current inequalities in terms of income amongst those who are employed on a full-time basis can be reduced;

- The need for affirmative action in terms of employment in order to reflect the demography of particular regions;

- The need to level the playing field in terms of business opportunities in order to address economic inequalities in terms of race amongst citizens in the consumer class;

- The need to level the playing field in terms of various forms of representation (in democratic structures, sport, international relations, etc.);

- The need for symbolic forms of restitution to address simmering tensions that undermine social cohesion in terms of race, class, employment, nationality, sexual orientation and religious affiliation.

Such interventions always entail the risk of unintended consequences and therefore have to remain open to revision. Here prophetic imagination and visionary leadership are required. Imagination has to come before implementation. For many, the biblical image of the jubilee year captures something of this vision, even though what that entails remains highly contested and even though such a jubilee can be nothing more than a new beginning on the road towards reconciliation. Indeed the jubilee year was supposedly announced on the Day of Atonement during the Passover feast (Kistner 1996:86).

Theological perspectives on the ultimate need for reconciliation with God

In certain contexts guilt may become absolutely overwhelming. There is no way in which reparation can ever be made, precisely given the lasting deficit. Justice cannot be done if justice would require that everyone should be given what is due to them. A relationship based on reciprocity can no longer be restored.

In interpersonal relationships murder may serve as an example, since a relationship between perpetrator and victim is of course no longer possible. In civil society there are several examples where it becomes hard to imagine how justice could ever be done. Consider Nazi guilt over atrocities committed during the Holocaust, the legacy of slavery and of colonialism, oppression during apartheid, or the impact of climate change on future generations. Here caution should be exercised, though: if the perpetrators are still in a position of political or economic power, reconciliation will not be possible if they do not do what can be done in terms of reparation and restitution. Likewise, if the beneficiaries (of apartheid) are still experiencing the benefits of economic oppression (whether they realise it or not), the legacy of the past will linger on and "national reconciliation" will scarcely be possible.[76]

In contexts where guilt is indeed overwhelming, it may become appropriate for Christian perpetrators to confess their indebtedness to Godself and not only to their victims. We may reach a point where we may also need God's forgiveness. In other contexts Christian victims may become so trapped in structures of debt (inequality), oppression and destruction that they can only cry to God for deliverance from evil. They may come to a point where they sense that only God can help them.

In yet other contexts where the line of demarcation between victims and perpetrators has become less vivid, the spiral of mutual accusations, of unwillingness to address the problem, of lethargy and anarchy, may be such that there would appear to be no way to escape a looming disaster. On a personal level one could consider broken marriages for which there seem to be no future, but also children and young adults who have become trapped in a culture of drugs, gangsterism, crime and prostitution. In South Africa there are ample instances in terms of criminality, unemployment, and the crisis in primary and secondary education. At a global level one could consider the deadlock in negotiations on climate change, where mutual accusations and the protection of vested interests preclude the progress that is required. How on earth can one break out of such an entanglement and not merely wait for the looming catastrophe to befall us?

---

76   In the words of Mahmood Mamdani (2000:183), "To reflect on the experiences of the TRC is to ponder a harsh truth, that it may be easier to live with yesterday's perpetrators who have lost power than to live with beneficiaries whose gains remain intact."

Can the Christian gospel perhaps offer hope for reconciliation in such contexts? Gregory Jones (1995:118) notes that "the restoration of our communion with God requires something beyond my repentance, beyond my initiative or any human initiative, but not beyond God the Father's gracious will for communion with Creation." This is the point where we need to realise the distinction between the church's ministry of reconciliation and what Christ has done outside us (*extra nos*) and on our behalf (*pro nobis*), and not only in us and through us (*in nobis*), once and for all (the *ephapax* of Rom 6:10). This is where we may recognise that we need not be burdened with doing God's work, that what holds the ecclesial community together is not common moral activity, that there is a fundamental asymmetry between divine and human action, an unbridgeable gulf between the work of Christ through which God reconciled the world to Godself (2 Cor 5:19) and our ministry of reconciliation,[77] a radical difference between God's forgiveness for "metaphysical guilt" (Jaspers) and our human way of forgiving someone else for some or other moral shortcoming,[78] between God's authority to forgive and the ecclesial powers to announce forgiveness on God's behalf (so widely abused in medieval indulgences). Indeed, as Miroslav Volf (1996:110) observes, any sense of final reconciliation is not the work of human beings, but can only be addressed through the new beginning offered by the triune God.

One may suggest that these very theological perspectives on reconciliation provide the source of inspiration and also a sense of

---

77 In a perceptive essay John Webster (2003:120) comments: "The church, therefore, lives in that sphere of reality in which it is proper to acknowledge and testify to reconciliation because we have been reconciled; in which it is fitting to make peace because peace was already made; in which it is truthful to speak to and welcome strangers because we ourselves have been spoken to and welcomed by God, and so have become no longer strangers but fellow-citizens."

78 Watts (2004:54) observes that, if we are implicated ourselves in the moral wrongdoing of others, it is difficult for any human being to forgive someone else. The would at least partially imply that one needs to forgive oneself. This raises the question of whether forgiveness can be extended at all, even in secular contexts, without underlying theological assumptions. Perhaps it is *only* God who has the authority to forgive, so that human acts of forgiveness are at best based upon God's forgiveness. It is indeed remarkable to observe how the inductive logic employed here raises theological questions if pursued rigorously.

accountability for Christians to engage in the ministry of reconciliation in church and society.[79] Because God has reconciled the world with Godself in Jesus Christ through God's Spirit, we can be reconciled with others irrespective of the differences that may divide us. On the basis of the cross and the resurrection of Jesus Christ there emerged the hope that injustices and enmity, even death and destruction do not have the final word. The indicative of God's forgiveness yields the imperative to forgive one another. This indicative is experienced as abundant grace that simply has to be shared with others.

Admittedly, "radical reconciliation" is best understood as an elusive mystery, a dream that cannot be fathomed or achieved. In theological jargon: it is an eschatological reality. The reality in ordinary human life and, alas, also in Christian communities is often very different. Yet this reality should not allow anyone to domesticate the vision of ultimate reconciliation. It is precisely this vision, juxtaposed with current realities, that provides the source of hope, inspiration and dedication to engage in the ongoing process of reconciliation, precisely in the midst of enmity, faction fighting and structural violence. If this eschatological vision of reconciliation is retrojected into the distant past, one can indeed do justice to the "re-" in reconciliation: to be together *again* – even where no such togetherness existed in the past. In a similar way the biblical vision of paradise may be understood as a vision for the future of a society that never existed before, that was retrojected into the distant past in order to indicate God's original intentions for the world.

It is in this context where the so-called deductive logic becomes relevant once again. It is remarkable to see how the three Christian ways of talking about reconciliation mentioned in the second section above are woven together in the Confession of Belhar accepted by the former Dutch Reformed Mission Church in 1986. This may also be an apt

---

79   In the RICSA report (see Cochrane, De Gruchy & Martin 1999:62-65) several aspects of the role of faith communities as reconciling communities were distinguished, namely aiding public processes of reconciliation, sharing resources with such aims, symbolic or liturgical actions and involvement in moral reconstruction.

quotation to conclude this contribution and to invite further exegesis of Article 3 of this confession:

> We believe that God has entrusted the church with the message of reconciliation in and through Jesus Christ; that the church is called to be the salt of the earth and the light of the world that the church is called blessed because it is a peacemaker, that the church is witness both by word and by deed to the new heaven and the new earth in which righteousness dwells.

> [We believe] that God's life-giving Word and Spirit has conquered the powers of sin and death, and therefore also of irreconciliation and hatred, bitterness and enmity; that God's life-giving Word and Spirit will enable the church to live in a new obedience which can open new possibilities of life for society and the world;

> [We believe] that the credibility of this message is seriously affected and its beneficial work obstructed when it is proclaimed in a land which professes to be Christian, but in which the enforced separation of people on a racial basis promotes and perpetuates alienation, hatred and enmity; that any teaching which attempts to legitimate such forced separation by appeal to the gospel, and is not prepared to venture on the road of obedience and reconciliation, but rather, out of prejudice, fear, selfishness and unbelief, denies in advance the reconciling power of the gospel, must be considered ideology and false doctrine.

> Therefore, we reject any doctrine which, in such a situation sanctions in the name of the gospel or of the will of God the forced separation of people on the grounds of race and colour and thereby in advance obstructs and weakens the ministry and experience of reconciliation in Christ.

Bibliography

Ackermann, Denise 1996. "On hearing and lamenting: Faith and truth-telling". In: Botman, HR & Petersen, RM (eds): *To remember and to heal: theological and psychological reflections on truth and reconciliation*, 47-56. Cape Town: Human and Rousseau.

Alberts, Louw & Chikane, Frank (eds) 1991. *The road to Rustenburg*. Cape Town: Struik.

Arendt, Hannah 1959. *The human condition: A study of the central dilemmas facing man.* Garden City: Doubleday.

Asmal, Kader, Asmal Louise & Roberts, Ronald Suresh 1997. *Reconciliation through truth: A reckoning of apartheid's criminal governance.* Cape Town: David Philip.

Balcomb, Anthony 1988. "The N.I.R. – Context, message and theology". In: Nürnberger, Klaus & Tooke, John (eds): *The cost of reconciliation in South Africa: NIR Reader 1*, 131-142. Cape Town: Methodist Publishing House.

Baum, Gregory & Wells, Harold (eds) 1997. *The reconciliation of peoples: Challenges to the churches.* Maryknoll: Orbis Books.

Boesak, Allan & DeYoung, Curtiss 2012. *Radical reconciliation: Beyond political pietism and Christian quietism.* Maryknoll: Orbis Books.

Boesak, Willa 1996. "Truth, justice, reconciliation". In: Botman, HR & Petersen, RM (eds): *To remember and to heal: theological and psychological reflections on truth and reconciliation*, 65-69. Cape Town: Human and Rousseau.

Bonhoeffer, Dietrich 1996. *Life together.* Minneapolis: Fortress Press.

Bosch, David J 1980. *Witness to the world: The Christian mission in theological perspective.* Atlanta: John Knox Press.

Bosch, David König, Adrio & Nicol, Willem (reds) 1982. *Perspektief op die ope brief.* Pretoria: Human & Rousseau.

Bosch, David J 1975. "The church as the 'alternative community'". *Journal of Theology for Southern Africa* 13, 3-11.

Bosch, David J 1986. "Processes of Reconciliation and Demands of Obedience: Twelve theses". In: Thlagale, B & Mosala, Itumeleng J (eds): *Hammering swords into ploughshares*, 159-171. Johannesburg: Skotaville Publishers.

Botha, Johan G 1989. "Struggling with the confession of guilt – Recent developments within the SACC". In: Finca, Bongani *et al.* 1989. *Confessing guilt in South Africa: The responsibility of churches and individual Christians.* Braamfontein: SACC.

Botha, Johan G 1989. *Skuldbelydenis en plaasbekleding, Teks en Konteks 5.* Bellville: Universiteit van Wes-Kaapland.

Botha, Nico 1998. "Why we have confessed". In: Du Toit, Cornel W (ed): *Confession and Reconciliation: A Challenge to the Churches in in South Africa*, 17-23. Pretoria: Unisa.

Botman, H Russel 1999. "The offender and the church". In: Cochrane, James, De Gruchy, John W & Martin, Stephen (eds): *Facing the truth: South African faith communities and the Truth and Reconciliation Commission*, 126-131. Cape Town: David Philip.

Botman, H Russel & Petersen, Robin M (eds.) 1996. *To remember and to heal: theological and psychological reflections on truth and reconciliation*. Cape Town: Human and Rousseau.

Brümmer, Vincent 2005. *Atonement, Christology and the Trinity: Making sense of Christian doctrine*. Aldershot: Ashgate.

Brümmer, Vincent 2007. "Farrer, Wiles and the Causal Joint". In: *Brümmer on meaning and the Christian faith*, 283-294. Aldershot: Ashgate.

Cherry, Stephen 2004. "Forgiveness and reconciliation in South Africa". In: Watts, Fraser & Gulliford, Liz (eds): *Forgiveness in context: Theology and psychology in creative dialogue*, 160-177. London: T & T Clark International.

Cochrane, James, De Gruchy, John W & Martin, Stephen (eds) 1999. *Facing the truth: South African faith communities and the Truth and Reconciliation Commission*. Cape Town: David Philip.

Daye, Russell 2004. *Political forgiveness: Lessons from South Africa*. Maryknoll: Orbis books.

De Gruchy, John W 1988. "The struggle for justice and ministry of reconciliation". In: Nürnberger, Klaus & Tooke, John (eds): *The cost of reconciliation in South Africa: NIR Reader 1*, 166-180. Cape Town: Methodist Publishing House.

De Gruchy, John W 1989. "Confessing guilt in South Africa today". In: Finca, Bongani *et al., Confessing guilt in South Africa: The responsibility of churches and individual Christians*. Braamfontein: SACC.

De Gruchy, John W 1993. "Guilt, amnesty and national reconciliation: Karl Jaspers' *Die Schuldfrage* and the South African debate". *Journal of Theology for Southern Africa* 83, 3-13.

De Gruchy, John W 2002. *Reconciliation: Restoring justice*. Minneapolis: Fortress Press.

Dowdall, Terry 1996. "Psychological aspects of the Truth and Reconciliation Commission". In: Botman, HR & Petersen, RM (eds): *To remember and to heal: theological and psychological reflections on truth and reconciliation*, 27-36. Cape Town: Human and Rousseau.

Du Toit, Cornel W (ed) 1998. *Confession and Reconciliation: A Challenge to the Churches in in South Africa*. Pretoria: Unisa.

Everett, William Johnson 1999. "Going public, building covenants: Linking the TRC to theology and the church". In: Cochrane, James, De Gruchy, John W &

Martin, Stephen (eds): *Facing the truth: South African faith communities and the Truth and Reconciliation Commission*, 153-163. Cape Town: David Philip.

Finca, Bongani *et al.* 1989. *Confessing guilt in South Africa: The responsibility of churches and individual Christians*. Braamfontein: SACC.

Gerwel, Jakes 2000. "National reconciliation: Holy Grail or secular pact?" In: Villa-Vicencio, Charles & Verwoerd, Wilhelm (eds): *Looking back: Reaching forward*, 280-286. Kenwyn: University of Cape Town Press.

Grunebaum-Ralph & Stier, Oren 1999. "The question (of) remains: Remembering Shoah, forgetting reconciliation". In: Cochrane, James, De Gruchy, John W & Martin, Stephen (eds): *Facing the truth: South African faith communities and the Truth and Reconciliation Commission*, 142-152. Cape Town: David Philip.

Hay, Mark 1998. *Ukubuyisana: Reconciliation in South Africa*. Pietermaritzburg: Cluster Publications.

Institute for Contextual Theology 1986. *The Kairos Document: Challenge to the church*, revised second edition. Johannesburg: Institute for Contextual theology.

Jones, Gregory 1995. *Embodying forgiveness: A theological analysis*. Grand Rapids: WB Eerdmans.

Kinnamon, M 2003. *The vision of the ecumenical movement and how it has been impoverished by its friends*. St Louis: Chalice.

Kistner, Wolfram 1996. "The biblical understanding of reconciliation". In: Botman, H Russel & Petersen, Robin M (eds): *To remember and to heal: theological and psychological reflections on truth and reconciliation*, 79-95. Cape Town: Human and Rousseau.

Linden, Ian 1997. "The church and genocide: Lessons from the Rwandan tragedy". In: Baum, Gregory & Wells, Harold (eds): *The reconciliation of peoples: Challenges to the churches*, 43-55. Maryknoll: Orbis Books.

Maluleke, Tinyiko S 1999. "The Truth and Reconciliation discourse: A black theological evaluation". In: Cochrane, James, De Gruchy, John W & Martin, Stephen (eds): *Facing the truth: South African faith communities and the Truth and Reconciliation Commission*, 101-113. Cape Town: David Philip.

Mamdani, Mahmood 1996. "Reconciliation without justice". *Southern African Review of Books* 46 (December 1996).

Mamdani, Mahmood 2000. "The truth according to the TRC". In: Amadiume, I and An-Na'im, A (eds): *The Politics of Memory: truth, healing and social justice*. London: Zed Books.

Mkwatshwa, Smangaliso 1986. "Reconciling and restoring a divided church". In: Vorster, Willem S (ed): *Reconciliation and Reconstruction*, 57-69. Pretoria: Unisa.

Mofokeng, Thakatso A 1986. "Reconciliation and construction: Barth down to earth". In: Vorster, Willem S (ed): *Reconciliation and Reconstruction*, 34-48. Pretoria: Unisa.

Moltmann, Jürgen 2012. *Ethics of Hope*. Minneapolis: Fortress Press.

Mosala, Itumeleng J 1987. "The meaning of reconciliation". *Journal of Theology for Southern Africa* 59, 19-25.

Nürnberger, Klaus & Tooke, John (eds) 1988. *The cost of reconciliation in South Africa: NIR Reader 1*. Cape Town: Methodist Publishing House.

Nürnberger, Klaus 1988. "Costly reconciliation". In: Nürnberger, Klaus & Tooke, John (eds): *The cost of reconciliation in South Africa: NIR Reader 1*, 113-125. Cape Town: Methodist Publishing House.

Nürnberger, Klaus 1989. "Clarifying our concepts." In: Nürnberger, Klaus, Tooke, John & Domeris, William (eds): *Conflict and the quest for justice. NIR Reader No. 2*, 8-19. Pietermaritzburg: Encounter publications.

Schreiter, Robert 1992. *Reconciliation: Mission and ministry in a changing social order*. Maryknoll: Orbis Books.

Smit, Dirk J 1986. "The symbol of reconciliation and ideological conflict". In: Vorster, Willem S (ed): *Reconciliation and Reconstruction*, 79112. Pretoria: Unisa.

Smit, Dirk J 1995. "The Truth and Reconciliation Commission: Some tentative religious and theological perspectives". *Journal of Theology for Southern Africa* 90, 3-15.

Snyman, Deon (ed.) 2012. *Restitution Toolkit*. Cape Town: Restitution Foundation.

Swartz, Sharlene & Scott, Duncan 2012. "The restitution of personhood: An expanded paradigm for social justice and transformation in broken spaces." Unpublished draft paper.

Tutu, Desmond 1999. *No future without forgiveness*. London: Rider.

Villa-Vicencio, Charles 1995. "Telling one another stories: Towards a theology of reconciliation." In: Baum, Gregory & Wells, Harold (eds): *The reconciliation of peoples: Challenges to the churches*, 30-42. Maryknoll: Orbis Books.

Villa-Vicencio, Charles 2002. *The Art of Reconciliation*. Ostervala: Life & Peace Institute.

Volf, M 1996. *Exclusion and embrace: A theological exploration of identity, otherness, and reconciliation*. Nashville: Abingdon Press.

Watts, Fraser & Gulliford, Liz (eds) 2004. *Forgiveness in context: Theology and psychology in creative dialogue*. London: T & T Clark International.

Watts, Fraser 2004. "Christian theology". In: Watts, Fraser & Gulliford, Liz (eds): *Forgiveness in context: Theology and psychology in creative dialogue*, 50-68. London: T & T Clark International.

Webster, John 2003. "The ethics of reconciliation". In: Gunton, Colin (ed): *The theology of reconciliation*. London: T & T Clark.

Weinstein, Harvey M 2011. "Editorial note: The myth of closure, the illusion of reconciliation: Final thoughts on five years as co-editor-in-chief". *International Journal of Transitional Justice* 5, 1-10.

Wink, Walter 2005. *Healing a Nation's Wounds: Reconciliation on the Road to Democracy*. Uppsala: Life & Peace Institute.

Ernst M. Conradie is Senior Professor in the Department of Religion and Theology at UWC, where he teaches Systematic Theology and Ethics.

2

LEARNING TO HEAR ONE ANOTHER IN ORDER TO RECONCILE OUR VIEWS

Mary Burton

In his novel *Homecoming* Bernhard Schlink has a character who explains why there will not be reprisals after German reunification, as he contemplates Berlin after the wall came down: "When you stay on, you have to get along". At its most basic, this can be a definition of reconciliation, simply to live together in one country without retaliation for past wrongs, in the hope of better options for the future, or even in the absence of other alternatives.

Yet, if we are to invoke reconciliation as a "guiding vision" for South Africa, as a realistic goal and not only a dream, we must define it more ambitiously than that.

Ernst Conradie's paper traces some of the ongoing debates, and cites others for further consideration, aiming for conceptual clarity. Even with this as a yardstick, the term is so widely and differently used that a generally accepted definition is not easy to grasp. One is reminded of Alice in Wonderland's Red Queen: "When I use a word it means what I want it to mean."

It may be useful to start by seeking agreement on what reconciliation does *not* mean. Frequently in public discussions a participant will raise the question of whether it means a return to some previously existing positive relationship, pointing out that such a relationship had not existed in South Africa. It is necessary to stress that this is not what reconciliation means in our current context.

It may well be that in some situations, where a healthy, loving, mutually beneficial relationship has broken down, but is subsequently healed and restored to something approximating its previous state, reconciliation can be said to have occurred. Something that was once good and desirable has been recreated.

In societal terms, however, the relationships that must be built are new and different. Reconciliation cannot mean a return to previous ways of relating to one another. It is necessary to dismiss the idea that the "re" in reconciliation means going backwards. The prefix can indeed sometimes signify a return, as in "re-establish" or "restore", or "recreate", but not in this case.

There are many other "re" words which give interesting insights, particularly with the significance of stressing or repeating an action: for example, reinforce, remember, reassure.

Reconciliation can also mean the bringing together of a set of facts so that they do not contradict one another, as in the reconciliation of financial accounts.

With this more positive interpretation of the word itself, what are the issues which would define the concept, one towards which all South Africans could aspire? I would suggest:

- Acknowledgement of a divided, unjust past;
- Willingness to cooperate in the interests of a better future;
- Recognition that peace depends on ensuring justice for all;
- Resolution of conflicts without violence;
- Building an inclusive society;
- Redressing, even eliminating, unjust inequality;
- Respect for different faiths and cultures, and an embracing of the richness of diversity.

There may well be others that could be the basis for reconciliation, giving hope to – and challenging – the country's citizens. Progress towards it, however, would be severely limited by the divisions and cleavages that still characterise society. South Africans in general do not know one another deeply; they lack true understanding of those who are different in language, culture and history; they do not communicate honestly and clearly with one another; they do not listen deeply to one another.

Therefore a prerequisite for seeking reconciliation is to develop a process of learning to listen across all sectors, creating opportunities and mechanisms for greater knowledge of self and of others. Being heard and understood, being truly seen and known, is a deep human need. It is the only way to transform toxic relationships.

Skills and strategies already exist to foster this process. What is needed is to spread the recognition of their importance, and to multiply their capacity in ways which will be relevant to a variety of situations and people.

When we are able to hear and absorb the experiences, needs and longings of others, we can start to work towards a reconciliation of our own and others' expectations, with the objective of working towards meeting them together.

Mary Burton was a commissioner of the South African Truth and Reconciliation Commission and a long-standing member of the Black Sash.

3

A DOUBLE-EDGED SWORD

Fanie du Toit

Reconciliation has its origins in theology but the concept has since travelled widely. Tracking its path through the volumes of material produced in psychology, sociology, philosophy and political science, to name but a few disciplines with dedicated reconciliation discourses, can be daunting. In the political arena alone reconciliation has become one of the most frequently used guiding concepts for countries in transition and more generally in post-conflict situations, along with other "high ideals" such as transitional justice, democracy and security.

Reconciliation's political rise in South Africa is largely a consequence of the country's transition since 1994, still regarded by many as a "world historic moment", as a prominent American peace-studies scholar recently put it to me. Popularly, reconciliation is invoked by politicians across the globe when calls are made for social cohesion or peace. It features prominently in international policy documents, such as the African Union's Post-Conflict Reconstruction and Development Policy framework, or the UN Secretary-General's report on Transitional Justice in 2004.

More locally, in dozens of African countries, reconciliation forms the conceptual backbone of national legislation and national institutional mandates aiming to deal with a violent past in favour of a better future. Apart from South Africa, several other African states such as Ghana, Sierra Leone, Liberia, Cote d'Ivoire, the Democratic Republic of the Congo, Burundi, Rwanda, South Sudan, Kenya, Zimbabwe, Mauritius, Morocco, Tunisia, Egypt, the Central African Republic and Uganda have all formalised reconciliation as national policy.

Reconciliation is written into countless civil society programmes seeking to effect "deep social change" after conflict. All this is true, despite many South Africans associating the term with an era of perhaps overly naive expectations at the onset of our democracy, and now feeling the time has come to shrug it off in favour of new social goals attuned more to the future than to the past.

This debate is far from over.

Clearly reconciliation's popularity is a double-edged sword. On the one hand, the pervasive presence of the concept makes it impossible to ignore. It is in no danger of disappearing from the public domain any time soon. In fact its public presence internationally is growing, despite its somewhat lower profile in South Africa twenty years after the end of apartheid. On the other hand, the term reconciliation often threatens to lose its meaning, or get co-opted – a point well-made in the discussion document that is included here. In some cases reconciliation is seen as the silver bullet that would solve all problems and absolve society and its institutions from seeking effective transformation

And so it is indeed important to inquire anew after the concept's origins, this time from the perspective of the unique demands of our times, both here in South Africa and further afield. The Institute for Justice and Reconciliation's South African *Reconciliation Barometer*, which tests South Africans' attitudes towards one another and the idea of reconciliation more generally on an annual basis (the project is now it is tenth round), seems to suggest that reconciliation retains important meanings for most South Africans and that the youth in particular are optimistic both about the future of reconciliation and about progress made so far.

This stands in contrast with the predominant public view that South Africa remains a deeply divided society, where "little has changed". Delving deeper into findings such as these may help us to establish those aspects of a democratic South Africa which have indeed worked and which have in fact brought about change, insufficient and disappointing as the total result may still be for many of us. It may help us to develop national development programmes based on careful analysis of our strengths, not only our deficits or weaknesses – an essential requirement for effective social transformation.

This approach would be in line with the discussion document's plea for a more inductive, rather than conceptual or deductive, approach – that is, learning from "the bottom up" what reconciliation may mean rather than approaching the task from a more abstract, theoretical vantage point.

There is another consideration which I would deem important for such an endeavour, namely to develop precise questions with which to study actual reconciliation processes in depth, not just people's opinions about them. The penny is dropping for social scientists in many parts of the world that talking about peace and reconciliation is not enough. Providing inspirational guidance at the onset of political transition is not sufficient. Normative guidance towards achieving social transformation ought to include more precise evaluative questions that could provide a frame of reference by which to determine utility, empirical recognisability and ultimately justification or explanation for the success or failure of processes facilitated in the name of reconciliation.

What could such questions be? Desiderata would include factors identified by political scientist Colleen Murphy, such as making clear the consistency of the concept across multiple layers of change in society, the normative significance of change invoked, and clear goals in terms of which to measure progress.

For me, these foundational requirements for the real-life evaluation of reconciliation could produce questions such as the following:

- What conception of reconciliation would be politically relevant and rhetorically effective in areas of intense and protracted conflict, as well as in an international arena largely dominated by the security paradigm of the "war on terror", rather than a more idealistic one such as those typically associated with reconciliation efforts? In short, how does one "sell" reconciliation in a tough political environment?
- How does one recognise national reconciliation processes once they are underway? How can one say one country is "reconciling" while another

is not, even if the latter claims to be? What are the empirical traits or minimum thresholds?

- What are the goals against which reconciliation processes ought to be judged, justified or evaluated?

For those of us in the "reconciliation business", these questions go beyond academic interest or even job satisfaction. They cut to the heart of the integrity of our work of seeking to build and restore relations in the wake of mass violence and the concepts that drive it.

Fanie du Toit is the Executive Director of the Institute for Justice and Reconciliation, based in Cape Town.

4

RESTITUTION: EMBODIED RECONCILIATION?

Why words are not enough

Sarah St Leger Hills

In my response to this far-reaching and thorough examination of reconciliation and its tributaries, I will concentrate on a tentative theology of restitution as it relates to the forgiveness/reconciliation journey. I posit that a Eucharistic model lends itself to a theological understanding of the forgiveness–restitution–reconciliation journey. As reconciliation is at the core of Christian life, so the Eucharist is central to the worship of God. It is the place where we come to find Christ, where "the body of Christ" meets together; where we give and receive this body; where we are reconciled once again and sent out in hope to love and serve the Lord. Forgiveness, prayer, lament, praise, hurt and healing collide in the holy mysteries of Christ's body.

> *Take, eat, this is my body which is given for you* (Church of England: Common Worship. Archbishops' Council 2012).

What does it mean to be the "body of Christ"? To share in this body? The concept of "body" as something lived in and living, as something which exists in relation to other bodies, as something which has different parts, as something potentially transformative as in the Eucharist, as integral to our lives on earth, is central to my paradigm of restitution within the reconciliation journey. It incorporates the ideas of community, of sacrament, of incarnation, of suffering, of healing. Bodies exist in real life. They can be hurt and healed, broken and blessed, given and received.

Restitution, like the body of Christ, is a gift. It is freely given and received. It is necessarily relational; its form is arrived at by both parties. In this way it is different from charity, which is given to, or even imposed on, the other. Restitution, like the Eucharist, points to a hopeful future, to a reconciliation which is from God, with God and each other. It leads to the possibility of a shared future, in the reality of a relationship once broken. It involves the giving and receiving of something actual, concrete, embodied. In that moment of administration of the communion, of the giving and receiving of the body and blood of Christ, the door of grace opens. This is not a private event – it occurs within a community, witnessed by that community, prepared for together and sent out as one into the world. It is not a one-off happening – we are fed again and again by this body and blood, we remember, give thanks, celebrate, offer ourselves not once, but over and over again.

Reconciliation between each other, likewise, is communal. It, at best, needs to be embodied, communal, public and ongoing. It is a process, a journey, a movement. It means getting to know "the other", making a commitment to continue on the road together.

Christ is present in the mystery of the Eucharist. Restitution is perhaps the most "human" part of the reconciliation journey – potentially mundane, at least "ordinary". George Herbert's poem *Prayer* speaks of "heaven in ordinary" – perhaps a metaphor for what is happening in the process of restitution within reconciliation; as also within the "ordinariness" of the bread and wine in the Eucharist. These ordinary things – the actual, practical, concrete restitutive object or action, and the everyday food shared at the communion rail – are both transformed and transformative in the sacramental setting of reconciliation – whether the reconciliation is in the world or the church; whether it takes place in a township shopping centre or at an altar within a communion service. Both involve the people of God, the body of Christ. Both involve a grace-filled act. Both summon the ordinary and transform it into hope. Both enable an ongoing and reconciliatory relationship.

The main tenets behind my theology of restitution, that of a grace-filled and sacramental sharing of gifts, thus allow a conversation between the concepts of word and sacrament, which leads towards a possible re-reading of the Eucharist as the model for the restitution process. As the Eucharist is the union of word and sacrament, so reconciliation is the union of forgiveness and restitution. Forgiveness thus can be viewed as Word, and restitution as Sacrament, an outward and visible sign of the Word. Both are necessary for reconciliation, in the same way that both Word and Sacrament are crucial for the Eucharistic service liturgically and theologically.

So restitution envisaged as an outward and visible sign of God's grace through Christ, which is the outward sign of that inward grace of forgiveness, leads to a restoration of relationship with God, and therefore with each other. Reconciliation then can be understood, can be seen to have occurred, or be occurring, when that inward or inner theological and psychological working of forgiveness takes place, and is shown outwardly to have occurred by the "sacramental" act of restitution. Just as Word and Sacrament bring embodied hope and reconciliation with God in the Eucharist, so forgiveness and restitution bring reconciliation with "the other", and thus hope for the future. This can be seen both on an individual level and on a community or societal level.

Without restitution, it is potentially hard to truly take part in a grace-filled and hopeful reconciliation, just as we are reminded in the Eucharist of Christ's presence among us. In the service of the Word, the Scriptures are read and interpreted to us without our being able to taste and see, as forgiveness is an internal process, which even if spoken, may be hard to grasp. The Sacrament of the bread and wine, the body and blood, however, is seen, involves action, and is embodied. The act of restitution is seen, practical and embodied. Reconciliation follows as the culmination of both processes. Restitution without forgiveness is not possible in a true relational sense, as the Sacrament of the bread and wine must be rooted in Scripture, and so is not possible without reference to the Word of God.

As reconciliation is not a "one-off" process, we need to revisit the Eucharist time and again, to both continue our journey towards God, and celebrate and commemorate His reconciling presence among us. Likewise, it may be necessary to revisit forgiveness and restitution in order to continue our journey towards reconciliation. The crux of the process occurs at the moment of giving and receiving the Eucharistic elements, in the movement from God in God's gift of grace towards us; and then the movement between each other as the body of Christ is given and received. The act of giving or receiving the body of Christ, the bread, is concrete, material, a movement towards "the other". When thinking about the act of restitution, this too is concrete, material, an actual movement towards "the other". David Brown (2011:390) notes that the Christian faith is not exclusively a religion of the word:

> [B]ody is no less integral to who we are than the words that express our minds Indeed, in choosing the visual symbols of bread and wine to represent his own presence, Christ himself can be claimed to have endorsed just such a view.

I would take this further and argue that the idea of restitution is central to this bodily presence and the integral nature of this act in the Eucharistic liturgy. Without the giving and receiving of the body (and blood), the Eucharist is merely a service of word, not sacrament. Moreover, without the sacrament, reconciliation, one of the foremost purposes or products of the Eucharist, cannot be said to have taken place, or been fulfilled. Although of course it could be argued that the administration of the sacrament does not equate with the act of restitution, I would suggest that this is in fact the crux of the reconciliation journey in both Eucharistic terms and in human reconciliation – or in other words, in vertical (God to human) and horizontal (human to human) reconciliation. Without restitution, it is difficult to gauge the authenticity of the others' "sorry". Without the administration of the bread and wine, one cannot be said to have received communion, to have partaken of the holy mystery that is the body of Christ. In both cases reconciliation is surely at best partial, if not wholly absent. Herbert McCabe (2010: xii) writes that Christ's

> ... risen body is the foundation of the new human race. Already, moreover, we can belong to the new creation, not yet physically but sacramentally; our bodies make contact, real contact, with the risen Christ through mysteries, symbols in which he is present to us.

McCabe goes on to argue that in the mysteries we are not only in the presence of the risen Christ, but we are also "able to be really present to each other." And that

> ... the sacraments can be regarded as mysteries of human community. As symbolizing the union in the Spirit between men which they bring about, as well as mysteries of Christ's action or his bodily presence (McCabe 2010: xii).

This speaks to the idea of restitution as an integral part of the process of reconciliation – that in the restitutive giving and receiving of the symbolic body, reconciliation between and within communities can occur.

It is thus in the physical nature of the bread and wine, "the body and blood of Christ", that the presence of Christ can be seen, touched, tasted. This embodiment is what allows us to make real for ourselves the logos, and in so doing confirms beyond doubt the movement towards reconciliation. This outward and visible sign of God's grace, given and received, thus puts restitution at the heart of the reconciliation process.

As in the action of the administration of the bread and wine, the two-way act of giving and receiving, so the action of restitution is a mutual process. By this I mean that, unlike charity, which is a one-way action, restitution must be arrived at by both parties, i.e. the perpetrator and the victim as part of their ongoing journey have to decide together what form appropriate restitution might take. Charity is handed down from the giver to the needy, and is generally a gift which is thought to be appropriate by the giver, rather than arrived at after discussion with the recipient. In the case of restitution, both parties gain some power, and also, importantly, both take some responsibility for the nature of the restitution and the ongoing reconciliatory relationship.

Jesus did not commend us to remember him with words alone. Of course, one cannot argue that Jesus gave us physical elements to use to remember, to give thanks, to be healed and reconciled with, purely in preference to words alone. The Eucharist has at its root the Passover meal; the remembrance of the many times Jesus sat and ate with tax collectors and sinners; the offering and acceptance of peace and hospitality. However, the symbolism of food in the Eucharist is more than these. It is also the embodiment of Jesus in his incarnation; the acknowledgement of the human need to touch, to experience with our bodies, in order to believe. In the Eucharist we are able to touch Jesus' body in order to believe to receive the sacrament of grace which is being offered.

In linking this to the reconciliation journey, we see that it is in the embodiment of the "word", the remorse, the sorryness, the confession, that the wish for reconciliation can be believed. Restitution as outward and visible sign of this inward process or belief takes the form within the Eucharist of these consecrated elements. When these actual objects are given, experienced, touched, received, then the belief in a relationship that is truly healing can be trusted. This sacrament of restitution enables a hope-filled and reconciled future to become a realistic and potentially transformative reality.

> *We are the body of Christ. Although we are many, we are one body, because we all share in the one bread* (Church of England: Common Worship. Archbishops' Council 2012).

Bibliography

Brown, David 2011. *God and Grace of Body: Sacrament in Ordinary*. Oxford: Oxford University Press.

Herbert, George. "Prayer (I)". Accessed from www.poetryfoundation.org/poem/173636.

McCabe, Herbert 2010. *The New Creation*. London: Continuum International Publishing Group.

The Rev. Dr Sarah St Leger Hills practised as a psychiatrist, is currently a doctoral student in theology at Durham University, and also serves as an Anglican priest in the Diocese of Sheffield.

5

A THEOLOGY OF RECONCILIATION

The search for conceptual clarity

Demaine Solomons

The term "reconciliation" may be used both as a theological term ("reconciliation in Jesus Christ") and as a social term (the need for "national reconciliation"). The understanding of the social aspect of the theology of reconciliation as an ethical outpouring, a secondary result of personal salvation as opposed to an inherent aspect of reconciliation with God, has led to long-standing theological debates. Some theologians like Colin Gunton (2003) and John Webster (2003) believe that emphasising a social dimension to the theology of reconciliation will lead to a decreased understanding of the transcendent nature of Christ on earth. On the other hand, theologians like John De Gruchy (2002) and Miroslav Volf (1996) believe that the horizontal aspect of reconciliation undeniably forms part of the vertical. They believe that there is a danger that reconciliation's social implications will be left to politicians, while its vertical ideals are explored theologically. On both sides of the debate, the bone of contention seems to be whether the primary emphasis should be on either a vertical or a horizontal understanding of reconciliation.

This leads me to two crucial questions: Are the social implications of the theology of reconciliation an ethical response to personal restoration with God? Or, is the horizontal understanding of reconciliation intrinsic to the vertical? The first question puts the social element of the theology at a lower level than the personal reconciliation with God. In other words, we are first reconciled to God, and as a consequence we alter our relationships in the world. The second question sees reconciliation with God-humanity and humanity-humanity as initiated, though not dictated, by God as one divine hope.

The point I would like to make here is that adhering to the intrinsic nature of reconciliation on a vertical and a horizontal level does not mean that human beings are slaves to the will of God, for not all of us shall choose to be reconciled with God and likewise will not choose to be reconciled with our neighbour. However, what is offered, to those who will accept it, is ultimate reconciliation through Christ's actions on earth and God's forgiveness. In this context the freedom to choose is still with human beings (even if one believes that God is still the initiator in the social scenario, for it is us who choose to act), but it places the whole of creation under a God-initiated mission of reconciliation, and thereby states that the divine hope of humanity's reconciliation with God is also the divine hope of humanity's reconciliation with one another.

The second point I would like to make concerns the various key concepts often used to describe a theology of reconciliation, including truth, justice, forgiveness and repentance. On closer investigation one becomes aware of the inherent tension between them. It appears that that truth and justice are often at odds with repentance and forgiveness. Truth, especially in cases of violent conflict, makes forgiveness very difficult. On the other hand, the fear of justice in its punitive form can make repentance rather complicated and can provoke one to ignore the importance of forgiveness. This tension has led theologians to define reconciliation in quite different ways, with some emphasising truth and justice, while others are more inclined to highlight forgiveness and repentance. It is important to note that justice and truth work together towards what David Stevens (2004:29-30) calls "forms of acknowledgment and accountability". Likewise, forgiveness and repentance may be described as having "collective and communal aspects". This suggests that the one group seeks freedom for the oppressed and oppressor, whilst the other group seeks peace by bringing the oppressed and the oppressor together. One may therefore state that we have two different understandings of the theology of reconciliation existing as one. According to the one, the focus is on liberating tendencies (truth and justice) with the goal of freedom, while the focus of the other is on reconciliation (forgiveness and repentance) with the goal of peace. One may also say that the goal of liberation is equality, while the goal of reconciliation is unity.

Taking such tensions into consideration, Robert Schreiter (2008:7) rightfully states that, "there is no formula or strategy for reconciliation that will be applicable in every instance." I believe that the practical application of these concepts is relative, for most people in South Africa and beyond would agree that there is no idea of perfect justice, or accurate truth. Likewise, it appears to be impossible to have the concepts of truth, justice, repentance and forgiveness existing in perfect balance, even while pursing reconciliation. As South Africans we are becoming more and more aware of this reality. Volf (1997:243) explains the use of the concept of truth: "[First] the belief in an all-knowing God should inspire the search for truth; the awareness of our human limitations should make us modest about the claims that we have found it ... We 'know in part,' second, because our limited knowledge is shaped by the interests we pursue filtered through the cultures and traditions we inhabit." On the point of truth, De Gruchy (2002:155) adds: "Given our human limitations, not least the partiality of our perspectives shaped by local location, past experience, loyalties, values and interests, as well as the nature of truth itself, we can never arrive at or grasp the whole truth." Both theologians agree that the meaning of the concepts used in a theology of reconciliation is relative to the particularities of one's social context. One may therefore argue that the contextual nature of the ideas of truth, justice, forgiveness and repentance places our understanding of reconciliation on a spectrum between the poles of liberation (truth and justice) and reconciliation (forgiveness and repentance).

These two groups of concepts, justice-truth and forgiveness-repentance, despite having different goals, are undeniably linked in any theology of reconciliation. Indeed, most theologians would insist that all four elements must be present for reconciliation to occur. For example, Stanley Hauerwas (1986:71) argues that "The issue is not whether there is a connection between salvation and social justice, but whether liberation is a sufficient image or metaphor to depict adequately the nature of that social salvation ... Part of our task, therefore, is to find other images as compelling as liberation to depict the salvation we believe accomplished in Christ."

To conclude, if one looks at the life of Jesus, on a horizontal and vertical level, Christ is seen as both a liberator through his actions for the poor and oppressed as well as a reconciler because of the sacrificial giving of his own life, but always with a hope for humanity to be reconciled with God. From a biblical perspective this can best be seen in terms of the two examples of the cleansing of the temple and Jesus' words of forgiveness to the soldiers whilst on the cross (see John 2: 13-16 and Luke 23: 34). On a vertical level, Jan Lochman argues that it is nearly impossible to understand the life and death of Jesus in terms of any one concept, be it liberation or reconciliation. This is because of what Lochman (1980:75) describes as the "multi-dimensional" nature of God's reconciliation with humanity. Salvation, he further explains, is the work of both a reconciling and a liberating God. If we therefore make the assumptions, based on the tensions within a theology of reconciliation, that the horizontal element is intrinsic to the vertical element of reconciliation, that truth, justice, repentance and forgiveness are the main concepts within a theology of reconciliation, that these main concepts are often grouped into liberating and reconciling tendencies, and that neither is alone fully capable of describing a theology of reconciliation, this may help us to see how these concepts function in public life.

Bibliography

De Gruchy, John W 2002. *Reconciliation: Restoring Justice*. Minneapolis: Fortress Press.

Gunton, Colin 2003. "Towards a Theology of Reconciliation". In Gunton, Colin (ed.): *The Theology of Reconciliation*, 167-174. London: T&T Clark.

Hauerwas, Stanley 1986. "Some Theological Reflections on Gutierrez's Use of 'Liberation' as a Theological Concept," *Modern Theology* 3:1, 67-76.

Lochman, Jan M 1980. *Reconciliation and Liberation*. Belfast: Christian Journals Limited.

Robert Schreiter 2008. "Establishing a Shared Identity: The Role of the Healing of Memories and of Narrative". In Kim, Sebastian, Kollontai, Pauline and Hoyland, Greg (eds): *Peace and Reconciliation: In Search of a Shared Identity*, 7-20. Aldershot: Ashgate.

Stevens, David 2004. *The Land of Unlikeness: Explorations into Reconciliation*. Dublin: Columba Press.

Volf, Miroslav 1996. *Exclusion and Embrace: A Theological Exploration of Identity, Otherness and Reconciliation*. Nashville: Abingdon Press.

Webster, John 2003. "The Ethics of Reconciliation". In Gunton, Colin (ed): *The Theology of Reconciliation*, 109-124. London: T&T Clark.

Demaine Solomons is a PhD student at the VU University in Amsterdam and is a part-time lecturer in the Department of Religion and Theology at UWC.

6

REDISCOVERING RECONCILIATION

A Response to the Call for Reconciliation as a Governing Symbol in Post-1994 South Africa

Vuyani S. Vellem

Introduction

In this paper I argue that the quest for conceptual clarification of reconciliation in South Africa is not adequate on its own without the category of experience. If one takes the question of the deficit in relation to reconciliation as articulated in the position paper by Ernst Conradie, it becomes necessary first and foremost for a black theology of liberation as a whole to be interpreted as a response to the ever-residual deficiencies of redress after unfathomable, unquantifiable extremes of human degradation by racial discourses that dominated our South African history for over three centuries to date. Indeed, as the position paper correctly argues, some of the tragic losses emanating from the dismembered body of a black African at the encounter with a white, racist and masochistic culture of modernist domination cannot and will never be repaid. There will always be a deficit.

Nonetheless, it would be erroneous to equate a black theology of liberation to a discourse intended to deal with maximum, permanent extremes of loss and damage without being attentive to the permanence of the deficit in the lives of its interlocutors. Indeed, it would probably be intrinsic and original to a reductionist discourse that never accorded black Africans a sense of humanity in its fullness. I will pursue these issues quite briefly in this response. I interrogate the notion of deficit, engage the epistemological rationality of conceptual analysis, and conclude by pointing to the need to draw from African jurisprudence if we are to find reconciliation in South Africa.

The notion of the deficit and a black theology of liberation

My response focuses specifically on the discussion of reparation and the notion of a deficit. I am particularly fascinated by this exposition and agree that the discrepancy that arises from an act of wrongdoing implies some form of deficit: "a deficit that can never be undone". A derivative of calculative rationality, namely financial calculation according to Conradie, this notion implies that anything associated with wrongdoing that cannot be counted or calculated and therefore compensated financially is a deficit. The following sentiments encapsulate the matter at stake:

> In the context of long-lasting conflicts between groups, this notion of a deficit becomes far more entangled. The economic, social and educational impact of centuries of imperialism, slavery, colonialism and apartheid in South Africa created an immense deficit. Two decades after the transition to a democratic dispensation this deficit is undoubtedly still felt by many "previously disadvantaged" citizens, often with considerable resentment and anger (see page 43).

Nothing could be truer concerning our current South African situation. However, I must caution that when the sentiments above are confined to the meaning of the deficit as defined by Conradie, one might be tempted to imagine that such a deficit – wrongdoing that cannot be undone – speaks to the incalculable impact of imperialist socio-economic, racist, colonial exclusions and apartheid. Yes, that might be the case, but it is much more nuanced, as I shall attempt to demonstrate in this paper. Conradie deals with this possible error – the error of equating the immensity of the deficit with the long-lasting conflicts – by making a brilliant distinction between the need for reparation and dealing with the lasting deficit.

Accordingly, this distinction entails that reparation only serves the type of wrongdoing that can be undone, meaning that it can be calculated, while in contrast the deficit cannot be measured. If we pursue this line of thinking to some of its logical implications, the quagmire of the symbol of reconciliation in South Africa becomes vivid.

Firstly, I am in full agreement with Conradie about the distinction between reparation and dealing with the deficit. Reparation implies the measurability of imperial, racist socio-economic and political damages that can be undone, i.e. the impact of these ills that can be measured. In other words, notwithstanding the limitation of measures, or criteria that could be utilised to calculate these damages, it is not implausible to subject these damages to a calculative rationality.[1] I contend that the Truth and Reconciliation Commission (TRC) is one example *par excellence* that has been instituted in South Africa to measure such damages. Yes indeed, the choices that were made – without even getting into the merits of the choices themselves – had to be subjected to measurability and calculation. In our South African context, therefore, it is not the immeasurability of reconciliation *per se* that seems to have been the problem, but the *deficient* calculations and measures adopted to deal with reparation. In terms of the measurability of the damages and the woundedness of our nation, the impact of the TRC has been extremely minimalist. My first point is that the effects and impact of imperialism, colonialism and apartheid which are still felt in post-1994 South African public life, albeit long-lasting, could plausibly be subjected to a calculative rationality.

Secondly and directly related to the first point above, if the logic of calculation is pushed to its maximum – that is, if we concede that there could be minimum and maximum prongs of calculation – how then do we go beyond this logic even if the maximum calculation is attained? If we accept that there is a limit to this calculative rationality, no matter how far it could be stretched, then we need to accept that reparation

---

1   There are many examples for this, especially after the incalculable damage of World War II. The establishment of the Israeli state and the reconstruction of Germany after the war show that some measures of compensation were arguably fair and just.

could reach a realm that is no longer calculable and assume a deficit that is permanent and immeasurable. The issue therefore is how these two prongs of measurability and immeasurability are to be employed to interpret our situation.

We need to understand that the notion of a deficit connotes that which cannot be undone, whether immense or minute. Within the continuum of wrongdoing, proceeding from that which can plausibly be measured, a deficit would move beyond the realm of calculative rationality. In this sense the deficit also evokes the epistemological perspective of permanently flawed, residual damage emanating from wrongdoing.[2] In other words, the first important point to remember is that putting money as the prime measurement of life – that is, throughout the continuum of reparation and dealing with the deficit – has not only become hegemonic and dominant, but also aggressively defended in the 21st century. Obviously, money cannot be the only measure of the woundedness of our nation and *ipso facto* the only way in which reparation could be measured, given the limits of any form of calculative rationality. Within the realm of the measurable, money should not be the only instrument of measurement. This is where I think we should introduce a black theology of liberation and the epistemological perspective that it might contribute to addressing the calculable and incalculable dimensions of woundedness in South Africa.

A black theology of liberation, particularly its systematic articulation of faith, is often subtly dismissed as a discourse that is too preoccupied with the incalculable damage following the long-lasting conflict between black Africans and the West. This view assumes that a black theology of liberation is unable to disentangle our society from such residual

---

2   There are many works that have deeply examined the problem of instrumental rationality and modernity. The most recent is one by Ulrich Duchrow and Frank Hinkelammert, *Transcending Greedy Money* (2012). One of the most penetrating arguments they make has to do with the myths caused by this form of rationality, the distortions that are death-dealing as a result of the elevation of modernist calculative rationality into the whole of public life. A similar argument is made in Jürgen Habermas's analysis of society in advanced capitalism and in terms of his assertion about the "colonization of the life world" by the systemic imperatives of power and money.

damage, which includes permanent wounds that cannot be undone. It is often said that Black Consciousness was good, but that it was lacking in offering "practical solutions" to the myriad problems that we face in our country. Often practical solutions imply a calculative rationality, perhaps what might be designated as a form of pragmatism. I maintain that a black theology of liberation has consistently demonstrated its understanding of the impossibility of calculating the damage and wrongs that were perpetrated against the victims of imperialism, colonialism, and apartheid.

The various streams of a black theology of liberation that have evolved may be understood as implied responses to this challenge. It seems to me that it is not with reference to permanent losses arising from wrongdoing against black Africans (the lasting deficit) that a black theology of liberation has sought justice for its interlocutors – which would tend to make the goal of reconciliation impossible. I contend that the contribution of this school must be assessed in the light of the centuries of struggle exactly with reference to the calculable, measurable dimensions, without confusing the two prongs of measurable and immeasurable damage in the process. In other words, before we even venture into the deficit as defined in the position paper above, the focus should be on reparation in order to establish whether our commitment to reconciliation in South Africa succeeds in achieving the instrumental objectives of justice. I contend that the obsession of this school is not with how enlarged, immense, maximised and permanent the damage is, which cannot be calculated anyway and anyhow in our violent history. Instead, its focus is with the very minimum calculation in what is regarded as calculable damage – which may easily be distorted as incalculable. It is within the realm of the measurable that we must commence, a black theology of liberation would suggest. Indeed, in terms of the TRC discourse, reparations, which are conceivably measurable, reveal a picture that remains vividly skewed:

> The announced reparations strategy encompasses five categories: urgent need grants, annual pension-type grants of between R17 000 and R23 000, symbolic reparations, community reparations and institutional-reform reparations. It is estimated that these will cost

about 3 billion Rands – about 0.25% of the South African annual budget. It is perhaps instructive that what a "victim" will receive in an annual payout is less than what a commissioner now earns per month. Also, many of the perpetrators applying for amnesty have already received their "golden handshakes" from the government. A few victims' organisations and representatives have said that there was little consultation with the victims about the type and amount of reparations. Questions raised about the quantity and quality of reparations are often answered with the suggestion that "no amount of money can make up for the suffering of victims." One wishes that this argument would also be used with respect to the general financial cost of the TRC and its own "gravy train" ... – otherwise one detects a double standard (Maluleke 1997:340-341).

The issue in the quotation above is not about the immeasurability of reparation, but the skewed measurements of reparations for the victims. One wonders if at that point in our history the concept of reconciliation was unclear or not. The title of the article from which the sentiments above are cited is helpful for the argument I am advancing in this paper: "Dealing lightly with the wounds of my people" (Maluleke 1997). In other words, it is the minimalist and calculable measures that are accorded primacy in assessing the logic of justice in the reparatory discourse of the TRC. One could venture to generalise that a black theology of liberation responds to the *deficit* of all measurable truth, faith, interpretation, perspective and approach (in addition to money), and to the issues of justice, while the poor remain poor.

Apart from the saturation of pragmatism to which I have already alluded in South African public life and the elusive interlocution of theological discourse, it is the subtleties of persuasion, also in public discourse, that continue to undermine the measures that are required for reconciliation in South Africa. One such measure for reconciliation that seems to be widely underrated is justice. As I noted elsewhere,

> Too much emphasis on reconciliation, for example, might compromise justice and vice versa. By making justice subservient to reconciliation important tenets of justice may collapse and undermine the very reconciliation that might be sought to be achieved (Vellem 2012:351).

This means that without confining measurability and calculation to finances, there are other measures of reconciliation which are important. Xolela Mangcu (2012:277-278) rightly says:

> I have elsewhere argued that although Nelson Mandela played a pivotal role in ensuring our transition to democracy, he nonetheless left us the unfinished business of racism. Biko's challenge of the psychological freedom from racism was therefore left unaddressed by even the greatest political icon of the 20th century. In the effort to bring white people on board the project of democratisation, Mandela stopped short of challenging whites to change the attitudes that underpinned their privileged position in our society. Because of his emphasis on reconciliation, Mandela had "a rather generous interpretation of racism in South Africa".

Let me reiterate my point: the distinction between reparation and addressing the deficit entails that the former is calculable, while the latter remains incalculable, no matter the immensity of the calculable dimensions of the damages. The calculable cannot be measured in monetary terms only. This distinction between the calculable and incalculable dimensions of woundedness in our land has not been foreign to a black theology of liberation.

By focusing on the calculable aspects of reparation I have attempted to show that it is the minimalist, light dealings and subservient forms of justice and "generous interpretations of racism" that a black theology of liberation has been and will continue to be attentive to. What about that which is immeasurable? I suggest that we need to make a distinction between the metropolitan logic of cognitive clarity regarding reconciliation and the logic of experiential clarity regarding reconciliation.

The limits of cognitive clarification

The purpose of the position paper, as Ernst Conradie puts it, is to assist theological reflection "on the basis of conceptual analysis" of the notion of reconciliation in South Africa. True to its purpose, the overall timbre of this document is based on the clarification and verification of the concept of reconciliation surveyed through a nexus of paradigms. In other words, the quest for an intelligible conceptual essence, the quiddity of reconciliation is largely achieved through the nuances on reconciliation introduced by scholarship. What is absent therefore from any conceptual analytical framework? What is the epistemological gap? Akintunde Akinade (2012:108) provides an entry point to engage with the limits of cognitive conceptual analysis from a black theological perspective:

> Africa's theology of liberation takes the circumstances and conditions of African people seriously. It is a theological exercise that stems from praxis and critical engagement with the conditions that put people in bondage and oppression. The experience of the people become (sic) the *fons et origo* (source and origin) for theological reflection and engagement. This theological orientation is deeply rooted in the ghettos of human experience and condition.

The *fons et origo*, that is the source and origin of analysis in a black theology of liberation, is the experience of the people, the ghettoes of human experience among the non-persons. Conceptual analysis can only make sense if it is limited to what it really can offer as one of the means or vehicles to construct or reconstruct the requisite knowledge on reconciliation. I therefore see the exercise of conceptual analysis as a vehicle to achieving something else. This suggests that there should be a reason for employing it as a vehicle at this time in history in South Africa. While Conradie explicitly states that postgraduate students who work on reconciliation "require some conceptual clarification" regarding reconciliation and thus offers a reason for this exercise, I contend that there might be other reasons implicit in this exercise which are undisclosed. For example, the document states that "the validity of the term reconciliation as one expression of a guiding vision for the transition to a post-apartheid South Africa is not addressed", even though it is expressly assumed in my reading of the paper. The substratum assumed, or the subliminal assumption of the document is not addressed, but subsumed under the conceptual clarification of reconciliation. That substratum might be an allegiance to a particular epistemology and form of knowledge construction, even though there are others as South African history has hitherto shown.

Chinua Achebe once warned: "For when language is seriously interfered with, when it is disjoined from truth ... horrors can descend again on mankind" (in Akinade 2012:107). We cannot forget that the interference of imperial, colonial and apartheid language with the language of the oppressed of this country is attested by the horrors that descended on us throughout our history of conflict. In my understanding, speaking philosophically, conception is a product of apprehension and judgement.[3] We cannot go beyond the mental picture we require in order to fathom what reconciliation is all about. I doubt if abstraction could be the reason, or only reason, for the exercise proposed by Ernst Conradie. For this reason, I am turning around this question by arguing that the purpose of seeking conceptual clarity is limited only to the abstract verification of the concept of reconciliation and thus may not assist in discovering or recovering what reconciliation is in the experience of the non-person.

Furthermore, I argue that conceptual clarity on reconciliation has already been attained and is readily available, so that what we perhaps require is the discovery of reconciliation through experience more than abstract reflection on the meaning of reconciliation. We must be conscious in our choices that we do not uncover its reality and material existence and ipso *facto* continue to make it elusive. Conradie does make this point when he alludes to the role of Christian faith in dealing with the deficit. Nonetheless, the limits of abstract conceptualisation of reconciliation become crystal clear when any such quest proceeds with undisclosed interlocutors and paradigmatic contestations of knowledge construction in South Africa.[4]

It might be safe to assume that the postgraduate students at the University of the Western Cape are the interlocutors in this quest, but in the history of the struggle for liberation in South Africa a black

---

3   For some basic exposition on logic and its components, see Kiruki (2004: 113-116).

4   Cf. Vellem (2012). While in this particular work the role of interlocution and its apparent elusiveness is directed to a black theology of liberation itself, I also discuss the issue of reconciliation in relation to this.

theology of liberation identified the poor or the non-person as its main interlocutors and source for knowledge construction. The construction of knowledge within this paradigm follows what Itumeleng Mosala (2012:7-8) says through the words of Rose Dugdale:

> Revolutionary theory is not qualitatively on a level with bourgeois theory. It is methodologically distinct, because it can only be learnt, or taught, in the practice of organization. What is needed is to see a way to fight, and this cannot be taught in theory; it must be found and shown through practice.

The methodological problem of a conceptual analysis of the concept of reconciliation is its ultimate limitation in making sense of the impossibility of calculating the deficit. As a chosen starting point, rather than a reflection from the material acts of reconciliation in the praxis of the victims of imperialism, colonialism and apartheid, a conceptual analysis of reconciliation might seriously undermine and harm the benevolent gift of fragile reconciliation attained through nothing but a resilient gift of the deletion of the deficit by the marginalised. Reconciliation thus cannot be taught in theory, but must be found in practice – it is praxiological. This is the position I hold. Indeed, even if the interlocutors are the postgraduate students of the University of the Western Cape, their search for knowledge of reconciliation is methodologically inadequate when constructed only through conceptual analysis. Much more profoundly erroneous in such a quest might be the assumption that all postgraduate students at a university such that of the Western Cape share the same contours of interlocution in our history of the struggle and our goal for reconciliation.

Rediscovering and uncovering reparation and the notion of deficit

As indicated above, I doubt the suggestion that colonisation and systemic oppression cannot be calculated. Money is not the only measurement instrument available. The difficulty of reconciliation becomes apparent not by enlarging or expanding the amount or extent of the deficit, but ironically by focusing on that which is indeed calculable. When we focus on the calculable, we can establish how reconciliation itself has been minimised. It is the failure to respond to the "minimal calculations" that have defined the relationship between the perpetrator and the victim in our quest for reconciliation in South Africa. In other words, each time the victim minimises the calculable, the perpetrator may enlarge the incalculable, making it more complicated and therefore ultimately unclear what can be given back to the victim. Ernst Conradie says:

> The problem is that it is often not possible to distinguish so carefully between reparation, compensation and restitution precisely given the nature of the deficit. Relationships that have become distorted over a longer period of time are often more complicated than that. It is then no longer clear what can indeed be given back and to whom it should be given back (see page 70 above).

I think these sentiments adequately demonstrate the epistemological problem of calculative rationality when it is imposed on the incalculable. To cloud reparation with the nature of the deficit, or to use the deficit as a mirror of the reparation, raises important hermeneutical and epistemological questions. What is a serious problem here is that the incalculable becomes an odd measurement of that which is calculable precisely to maintain a minimalist perspective on that which can be measured and calculated, almost reducing it to nothing.[5] It might be apt to cite Conradie again at this point:

> What can be given back should be given back through acts of reparation. However, there is always a deficit that cannot be given back. This can still be addressed through acts of restitution ..., but even then a deficit will remain, if only because experiences of harm that was done can never be undone, only the impact of that harm can be addressed. Reconciliation is only possible if that deficit is forgiven by the victim (see page 67 above).

While I fully agree with this statement at surface level, it is nonetheless exactly at the point of forgiveness that our South African discourse

---

5   I have argued above that examples of reparation are readily available. If we proceed with the understanding of the deficit in the position paper, the difference between the Nuremberg trials and the TRC was with regard to the calculation package.

has hitherto failed! It has failed exactly because of our inability to see how forgiven we are, how minimal our response to those gracious interstices of forgiveness is, and how the deficit is slowly becoming toxic in our reconciliation because of our unresponsive attitude to the continuous disembowelment of the victim. There will always be a limit to reparation when deeds of harm perpetrated against others are a cause of permanent scars that are hard to undo. If we do not commence from the giftedness of forgiveness, there remains a gap, a gaping wound, a discrepancy, even if the impact of the harm is addressed. To address this gap, this discrepancy, is a *sine qua non* for reconciliation.

If reconciliation indeed becomes possible when the victim deals with a permanent gap or deficit that cannot be undone, what role does the perpetrator have to play? I assume that there are varied permutations to this thesis. One plausible permutation is already implied, namely where victims find themselves deleting this deficit on their own wherever they are, without the perpetrator ever reciprocating to address the burden borne by the victims for centuries. Note that the victim and the perpetrator cannot enlarge the deficit, because the deficit cannot be undone. The only recourse that makes the difference between the victim and the perpetrator is that the former can only assert how minimalist the reparation that is supposed to be worthy of the loss is, while the perpetrator may focus on how impossible it is for the deficit to be undone, thus suggesting that "we must move on" as is predominantly the case in South Africa. As Xolela Mangcu (2012:270-271) puts it, King Hintsa's ear is still missing today, after his brutal death at the hands of George Southey. Perhaps the deficit caused by his death has long been deleted and forgotten, but what about the ears that were taken as souvenirs? Are they "smaller" items that could not be brought back? The loss of the body parts of a deceased person has meaning for black Africans! At least Sara Baartman's body did come back. Most recently, we all know that up to this day, even though the Biko family might have forgotten about the tragic events of his death, the truth about the circumstances of his death remains elusive. The ears of King Hintsa remain missing as do many other calculable, measurable and tangible aspects of reconciliation.

The reader may set aside the buoyant sarcasm in the preceding thoughts and proceed to consider one of the most significant points about an African understanding of reconciliation discussed below.

Interstices to delete the deficit

I understand African jurisprudence to be inherently reconciliatory. One of the examples that I can give is the practice of *ukuhlawula ityala*, meaning the payment of damages when one impregnates a young woman. This practice prevails to this day. While there is some modification in the sense that males who father children now have to pay maintenance for their children, we should not confuse this with the practice of *ukuhlawula ityala*. This practice entails that a settlement for the act of impregnating a young woman is paid and that is the end! No matter how much we could try to undo the young lady's fate to be a parent, the damage is permanent, yet the penalty is not enlarged to the equivalence of permanent damage, but believe it or not, the penalty includes the deletion of the deficit itself. By the way, such an occurrence is not viewed as an act of failure only by the girl but also by the community. The child born in these circumstances remains in the family of the young woman, the victim, and the case is closed. If there is a possibility of marriage, then it is separated from the unfortunate occurrence, but often this implies that the two families are reconciled.

There are numerous other examples that I can mention. For example, when one's cow strays into another's cultivated lands and damages the crops, it is not the amount of damage that determines *ukuhlawula*, but the possibility of reconciliation when a penalty is paid. A symbol of contrition for the damage caused is often adequate to restore the relations between the two families. One of the most superb works which suggests that the jurisprudence of black Africans is inherently reconciliatory is Mqhayi's *Ityala la Mawele*. The work describes a conflict that arose as a result of the birth of twin boys and consequently the struggle to determine who was the elder of the two and thus the heir to the family. In the past twins were often killed, oral tradition tells us. When the twins were left to survive, many aspects in the social life of the

AmaXhosa were affected. The clan was almost divided into two as these two young men began to fight for the right to eldership and heritage in their home.

The details of the story are not important for now. The plot of the story is more important and that is the goal of reconciliation in every conflict, thus a jurisprudence that is inherently reconciliatory. To deal with this problem, the whole clan was involved, the hearings protracted, consultations were held, elderly people's views from distant places were sought, no condemning verdict was uttered, no stone was left unturned and ultimately life was saved and harmony restored.

In this case one has to understand that black African people do not equate the extent of the damage and thus the magnitude of the deficit as a standard for reconciliation. They have historically demonstrated this resilience in situations of vast discrepancies and unimaginable brutalities. By the way, Desmond Tutu already implied this when he spoke about the 'controversial' wealth tax in South Africa. John de Gruchy also penned an article for the *City Press* in support of Tutu's critique of a lack of magnanimity among the white sections of our population in South Africa to the gift and gesture of forgiveness by black Africans. He said:

> The Arch, as our dearly loved Volmoed Patron is known, has often made headlines. And, sure enough he did so again when *The Argus* blazoned across its front page: "Tutu: Tax wealthy whites!" The moment I saw the headline on the posters I knew that it had to do with the Arch's speech at the book launch in Stellenbosch the evening before.[6]

Once again, the issue here is not the amount, but the question of magnanimity and its morbid absence in public life since the demise of apartheid. The story of the TRC is an eloquent text of forgiveness, with gaping wounds and discrepancies whose harm cannot be undone.

---

6   See John de Gruchy's meditation of 25 August 2011 on the "Tutu tax proposal", published by Kairos Southern Africa, http://kairossouthernafrica.wordpress. com/2011/08/25/john-de-gruchy-meditation-on-the-tutu-tax-proposal/, accessed 9 May 2012.

I have attempted to show that the deficit has never been remote to Africans in their experience of conflict and reconciliation. It has never been the standard to measure reparation. Let me conclude this section by appealing to Beyers Naudé (in Hansen 2005:40):

> The concept of reconciliation also implies very clearly that to God this was meant not only as a verbal message to man, but that it had to become incarnate; an audible word that had to become a visible deed in the flesh before reconciliation could be effective. This was the price God was willing to pay – the Incarnation of Christ the Reconciliation of God with man. Do we realize what this implies: that all talk of reconciliation remains meaningless and even becomes dangerous if words are not transformed into deeds?

> Do we realize that our confession of faith becomes nothing but cheap talk, yes, becomes an act of hypocrisy if we do not fully accept and enact the reconciliation of God in our lives?

Any abstract view of the deficit goes against our theology of incarnation. It limits our ability to discover reconciliation in deeds and thus in the praxis of the poor. One cannot imagine how much of a settlement could ever be made if one fails to recognise that South Africa after 1994 simply survives to this day on the deficit that is ever deleted by the victims whenever it is enlarged!

Conclusion

Who does not grasp the conceptual meaning of reconciliation? I have argued in this response that the poor know it with their bodies. I suggested that it is not implausible to reverse the long-lasting deficits of our history by demonstrating how minimalist, light-hearted and gracious the interpretation of racism has been after 1994. I attempted to show that a conceptual analysis of reconciliation as a starting point might create opacity with respect to the material, tangible interstices of reconciliation.

After all, a black theology of liberation prioritises the lived experience of its interlocutors as the *fons et origo* for the construction of such knowledge. African jurisprudence is reconciliatory, as I have attempted to show. All I see following on the still missing ears of King Hintsa are the embodiments of reconciliation in the dismembered bodies of Andries Tatane, the Marikana tragedy, the Western Cape farm strikes, Zamdela in Sasolburg. Let us uncover the meaning of reconciliation in places where the deficit is deleted, otherwise its resurgence will be immensely toxic.

Bibliography

Akinade, Akintunde E 2012. "The Crucible of Faith: Justice and Liberation in the Work of Engelbert Mveng." *Religions* 3,106-135.

Duchrow, Ulrich and Hinkelammert, Frank 2012. *Transcending Greedy Money*. New York: Palgrave Macmillan.

Hansen, LD (ed.) 2005. *The Legacy of Beyers Naudé*. Beyers Naudé Centre Series on Public Theology. Stellenbosch: Sun Press

Kiruki, JK 2004. *Introduction to Critical Thinking*. Eldoret: Zapf Chancery Research.

Mangcu, Xolela 2012. *Biko: A Biography*. Cape Town: Tafelberg.

Maluleke, Tinyiko S 1997. "Dealing Lightly with the Wound of my People." *Missionalia* 25:3, 324-343.

Mosala, Itumeleng 2012. "The Role of Grassroots Organisations for Socio-economic Justice: Lessons from Beyers Naudé." Paper presented at ESSET's public lecture in Honour of Beyers Naudé, Johannesburg, 17 October 2012.

Vellem, Vuyani S 2012. "Interlocution and Black Theology of liberation in the 21st century: A reflection." *Studia Historiae Ecclesiaticae* 38, 345-360.

Vuyani S. Vellem is Director of the Centre for Public Theology and senior lecturer in the Department of Dogmatics and Christian Ethics at the University of Pretoria.

www.ingramcontent.com/pod-product-compliance
Lightning Source LLC
La Vergne TN
LVHW051648080426
835511LV00016B/2569